DISTANCE LEARNING

Principles for Effective Design, Delivery, and Evaluation

CHANDRA MOHAN MEHROTRA
College of St. Scholastica

C. DAVID HOLLISTER
University of Minnesota

LAWRENCE McGAHEY
College of St. Scholastica

Sage Publications
International Educational and Professional Publisher
Thousand Oaks ▪ London ▪ New Delhi

For information:

Sage Publications, Inc.
2455 Teller Road
Thousand Oaks, California 91320
E-mail: order@sagepub.com

Sage Publications Ltd.
6 Bonhill Street
London EC2A 4PU
United Kingdom

Sage Publications India Pvt. Ltd.
M-32 Market
Greater Kailash I
New Delhi 110 048 India

Printed in the United States of America

Library of Congress Cataloging-in-Publication Data

Mehrotra, Chandra.
   Distance learning: Principles for effective design, delivery, and evaluation / by Chandra Mehrotra, C. David Hollister, and Lawrence McGahey.
      p. cm.
   Includes bibliographical references (p.) and index.
   ISBN 0-7619-2088-9 (c) — ISBN 0-7619-2089-7 (p)
   1. Distance education—Curricula.   2. Education, Higher—Curricula.
3. Instructional systems—Design.   I. Hollister, C. David.   II. McGahey, Lawrence.   III. Title.
   LC5800 .M44 2001
   378.1'75—dc21   2001002978

This book is printed on acid-free paper.

02   03   04   05   06   07   7   6   5   4   3   2   1

Acquisition Editor:	Jim Brace-Thompson
Editorial Assistant:	Karen Ehrmann
Production Editor:	Sanford Robinson
Editorial Assistant:	Cindy Bear
Typesetter/Designer:	Tina Hill
Cover Designer:	Sandra Ng

Contents

Acknowledgments

In preparing this book, we have drawn on the ideas, theories, and research of colleagues from a variety of colleges, universities, institutes, and organizations who have developed creative ways to help students learn at a distance, raised important questions about effectiveness of instruction, and identified issues that need to be addressed. But most immediately, we are indebted to our own institutions, The College of St. Scholastica and the University of Minnesota, for the continuing opportunities to design and offer distance programs, to assess their effectiveness, and to use the findings for program improvement. Without these experiences, we could not have even thought about writing this book.

We are grateful to the members of the library staff at The College of St. Scholastica and the University of Minnesota. They demonstrated exceptional competence in providing us a large variety of reference materials in a timely fashion. The peer reviewers, Charles R. Geist, Betty Elliott, and Sharon B. Johnson, who read and critiqued the manuscript offered us valuable suggestions and pedagogical advice. We did our best to incorporate many of the ideas, suggestions, and insights they gave us, although by no means all; any remaining errors are ours alone.

Our families and friends offered us encouragement and assistance in many ways. Chandra Mehrotra wishes to acknowledge Indra Mehrotra, his wife and best friend, for her enduring support. He thanks their two children, Vijay and Gita, for their continuing interest in his work. He also thanks Nancy Bois for typing a substantial portion of the manuscript. David Hollister expresses deep appreciation to Georgiana Hollister, his wife and best friend, for her continuing support. David also wishes to acknowledge their three children, Patrick, Jonathan, and Martha, for their interest in his work on this project.

We had the good fortune to work with dedicated professionals at Sage. Jim Brace-Thompson initiated discussions about this project at the 1998 American Psychological Association convention where Chandra Mehrotra had organized a symposium on distance learning. This support and interest has been most gratifying throughout the process. It has been a pleasure to work with him. In addition, we appreciate the thoroughness of copy editor Alison Binder, whose knowledge about good writing enhanced the quality of the book.

Introduction

Distance learning, or distance education, is not a future possibility for which higher education must prepare—it is a current reality creating new opportunities and challenges for educational institutions; a reality offering students expanded choices in where, when, how, and from whom they learn; and a reality making education accessible to ever larger numbers of persons. Indeed, during the past several years, there has been a dramatic increase in the number of colleges, universities, and other providers offering distance education courses, workshops, and programs. A U.S. Department of Education report indicates that from 1995 to 1998, the number of institutions offering distance learning increased by 33%; during the same period, the number of distance courses and enrollments doubled (National Center for Education Statistics, 1999). Many observers believe that this growth is likely to continue. Why? Properly implemented, distance education can enhance the learning experience and increase access to higher education for a wide variety of potential students, especially those who have not been able to take advantage of the traditional on-campus experience.

Background and Audience

Although many institutions consider distance education a means of expanding their service area, addressing the needs of underserved populations, and developing new sources of revenue, it is the faculty's responsibility to make courses and programs available in new ways that are both effective and efficient. This effort requires rethinking the course design, selecting appropriate modes of delivery, creating strategies to engage students in active learning, maintaining contact with the students, and assessing student performance. In short, ensuring an effective learning environment in distance courses places new demands on the participating faculty, although many faculty members have had limited experience designing such courses. Likewise, college administrators need information to help them create the context and supports essential to deliver high-quality programs to remote students. *The special demands that distance education imposes on faculty and administrators prompted us to write this book.* Our goal is not to offer a comprehensive review of research on the subject but to provide a helpful guide for those with limited experience in designing, delivering, and evaluating distance learning courses and programs.

The book derives mostly from our individual struggles as teachers. We are always experimenting and trying to expand our repertoire of approaches to distance learning—sometimes successfully, sometimes not. We do not view ourselves as experts in technology. Instead, we are users of technology with a continuing passion for enhancing student learning—both in campus-based and in distance programs. When we are not sure of which technology would best help students achieve a given outcome, we draw on the expertise of technology specialists available at our respective institutions. Given this background and the continuing advances in technology, the book emphasizes principles, rather than details about specific pieces of equipment or software. The underlying assumption is that once instructors know what course content they plan to cover, what student population they expect to reach, and what learning outcomes they desire students to achieve, they can make technology-related decisions in consultation with the specialists who have the knowledge and experience related to a wide range of technologies. In other words, this is not a book on technology; it is a practical guide offering tips on launching a distance learning course or program. We intend this book to assist educators and administrators who are contemplating their initial involvement in distance education, discerning the extent of their commitment (from occasional courses to full degree programs), and choosing the modalities for delivering distance instruction.

We trust that this book will appeal to a variety of readers, from those already engaged in distance learning who want to further strengthen their current efforts to those who need background, guidance, and encouragement as a prelude to launching distance courses. The main audience for the book is faculty and administrators who are interested in exploring the implications of starting a program or are addressing an institutional mandate to launch a new program. Considering the increased interest in fostering student-centered learning, the isolation that many students experience in large classes, and the potential of technology to engage students in active learning, however, much of what we offer in this book can be applied to on-campus courses and programs as well. The challenge in both on-campus and distance programs is the same: how to put together an appropriate combination of activities, resources, and technologies to help each student achieve intended learning outcomes.

Overview of the Contents

Chapter 1 defines distance education and examines why many institutions of higher education are entering the field. We have elected to organize the remaining chapters of the text by considering what must happen before students enroll in a distance education course or program, what takes place while students are enrolled, and what transpires once students complete a distance course or program. With this organizing principle in mind, we offer an overview of the remaining chapters below.

Chapters 2 through 6 examine the planning and preparation stages of a distance education course or program. What needs to be done before students enroll?

Chapter 2 addresses strategies for attracting students to enroll in distance education courses and programs. Chapter 3 describes how we apply principles of good educational practice to distance education, including a discussion of strategies for improving communication, providing feedback, clarifying understanding of difficult concepts, and increasing student motivation. Chapter 4 focuses attention on designing a syllabus for a distance learning course, noting helpful features not typically found in the traditional classroom syllabus.

Chapter 5 describes and discusses the various distance education modalities more fully, including print, radio, audio conference, audio-cassette, television, satellite conferencing, interactive television, video-cassette, CD-ROM, Internet conferencing, and the World Wide Web. Chapter 6 enunciates various principles to consider in selecting the modes of delivery for distance education.

Chapters 7 through 9 examine implementation of a distance education program. What must occur while students are enrolled?

Chapter 7 explores ways to provide support services to distance students that are equivalent to those available to students on campus, such as library access, advising, tutoring, financial aid, and career services. Chapter 8 suggests strategies and tips for attaining high completion rates in distance courses without compromising educational standards. Chapter 9 focuses on assessing learning outcomes—ways to know whether students have actually learned through distance instruction.

Chapters 10 and 11 examine quality control in distance education. What must be done after students complete a course or program?

Chapter 10 explains how to monitor and evaluate distance programs to improve both implementation and outcomes. Chapter 11 addresses issues regarding accreditation of institutions offering distance learning programs and provides suggestions to help program administrators meet accreditation criteria.

To complete the text, we offer some concluding thoughts. The conclusion also addresses issues that were not included in earlier chapters and speculates about future directions in distance education.

Our Companion Web Site

Given the continuing growth of new knowledge regarding different aspects of distance learning and the level of detail that the constraints of available space place on a publication of this nature, we have included a number of references to Web sites throughout the book. We believe readers will find this information useful in keeping themselves abreast of new developments specific to their area of interest. Mindful of the rapid pace at which Web addresses change, new sites are created, and others become obsolete, however, we have opted to place most such information on the Web site accompanying the text, hosted by Sage Publications at www.sagepub.com/mehrotra. We trust this approach allows us to demonstrate better many points covered in the text. At the end of each chapter, we provide a general description of the pertinent topics that readers can expect to find at the Sage Web site. Examples of the material presented on the Web site include sample syllabi for distance courses; assessment strategies; updates on accreditation guidelines; links with relevant sites; and references to new articles, reports, and publications. This Web site will be updated at least twice a year for 2 years following publication of the book. We will appreciate receiving feedback regarding all aspects of the site; in addition, we invite readers to suggest resources for inclusion on the Web site.

Reference

National Center for Education Statistics. (1999). *Distance education at postsecondary education institutions: 1997-98* (NCES 2000-013). Washington, DC: U.S. Department of Education.

1

Distance Education

What Is It?
And Why Is It Expanding So Rapidly?

D istance education can be defined as *any formal approach to instruction in which the majority of the instruction occurs while educator and learner are not in each other's physical presence.* A wide range of instructional arrangements is encompassed by this definition. Indeed, distance education has existed for well more than a century, beginning with correspondence courses that were developed in the late 1800s. Lessons were mailed out, completed, returned to the instructor, graded, and then returned to the student along with the next lesson. Formal course credit (high school or college) could be completed in this manner, and eventually entire diplomas or degrees could be earned. This arrangement continues to the present, with a number of colleges and universities in the United States and overseas offering courses by mail.

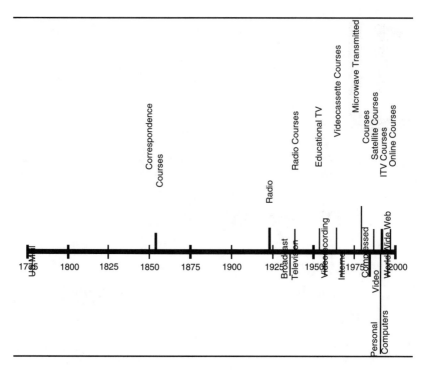

Figure 1.1. Timeline of Distance Education Technology

Impacts of Technology on Distance Education

In the 20th century, the gradually accelerating pace of technological invention led to many new forms of distance education (see Figure 1.1). Radio broadcast was adopted for course delivery in the 1930s. In some sparsely populated regions, individualized instruction occurred via two-way radio, for example, instruction to individual students living on remote sheep ranches in Australia. Not long after the arrival of commercial broadcast television, educational institutions began using it to deliver college courses. By the late 1950s, television channels dedicated to instruction had been established in many American cities. Later improvements in educational television included closed-circuit television, microwave transmission, video recording, and satellite transmission. Video recordings of lectures and other materials were mailed to students. Satellite and microwave television were supplemented with telephone links to enable two-way audio interaction.

Interactive Television

More recently has come the widespread adoption of fully interactive television (ITV), facilitated by the invention of *compressed video,* which could use existing copper telephone lines for transmission, and later, by the enormous growth of networks of fiber-optic cable, which permits the transmission of higher-quality video images. By the 1990s, the costs of equipping classrooms for television transmission had dropped substantially and had come within reach of many educational institutions. The instructor's site and the students' site could each readily transmit audio and video to the other. Instruction could be fully interactive. The availability of full interactivity for distance education persuaded many otherwise skeptical educators and administrators to give serious consideration to establishing distance courses and programs. Prior to full interactivity, distance education had often been considered "second choice" and somewhat suspect. By the late 1990s, many institutions of higher education were offering entire degree programs through ITV.

The Internet and Distance Education

Meanwhile, by the mid-1990s, the digital revolution had developed the personal computer, the Internet, the World Wide Web ("www" or "the Web"), and the CD-ROM to the point where it became feasible to deliver educational content directly to students' homes and offices. Interaction of students with each other and with the instructor can now be synchronous (occurring simultaneously) or asynchronous (occurring at different times), with the latter providing additional flexibility in students' and instructors' schedules. Geographic location ceased to be a major consideration in that Web-based courses could be taken anywhere an Internet connection existed and any time of the day or night.

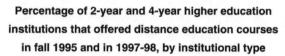

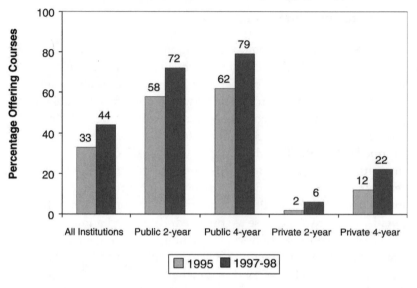

Figure 1.2. Percentage of Institutions Offering Distance Education

SOURCE: From *Distance Education at Postsecondary Education Institutions 1997-98* (p. 48), by National Center for Education Statistics, 1999, Washington, DC: U.S. Department of Education.

NOTE: This is the only figure that includes information for private 2-year institutions.

The Prevalence of Distance Education in the United States

The last few years have seen an enormous growth in the number of higher education institutions offering distance courses. As shown in Figure 1.2, in 1998 (the latest year for which figures are available), 44% of all 2-year and 4-year higher education institutions offered distance courses, compared with 33% in 1995 (National Center for Education Statistics, 1999).

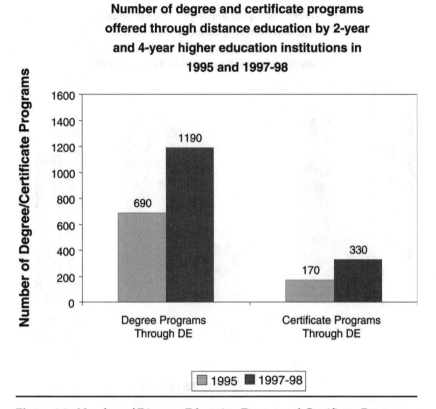

Figure 1.3. Number of Distance Education Degree and Certificate Programs
SOURCE: From *Distance Education at Postsecondary Education Institutions 1997-98* (p. 51), by National Center for Education Statistics, 1999, Washington, DC: U.S. Department of Education.

Likewise, the number of degree programs offered through distance education increased from 690 in 1995 to 1,190 in 1997-1998 (see Figure 1.3). An additional 20% of the institutions surveyed planned to start distance education programs within 3 years (National Center for Education Statistics, 1999). The growth between 1995 and 1998 appears to have occurred in use of the Web for distance learning, rather than with ITV or one-way prerecorded video. Use of the latter two modes actually declined slightly, as illustrated in Figure 1.4. Many observers believe that the growth in distance education in the years ahead will continue to occur primarily through the use of Web-based courses.

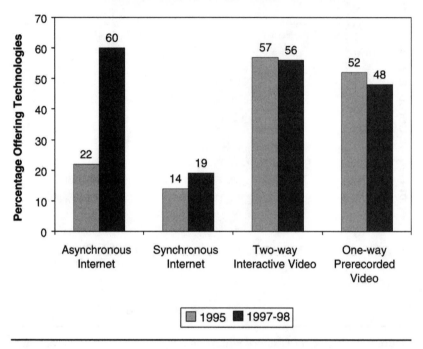

Percent of 2-year and 4-year higher education institutions offering distance education courses that used various types of technologies to deliver distance education courses in 1995 and 1997-98

Figure 1.4. Technologies Used in Distance Education in 1995 and 1997-1998
SOURCE: From *Distance Education at Postsecondary Education Institutions 1997-98* (p. 52), by National Center for Education Statistics, 1999, Washington, DC: U.S. Department of Education.

Societal Changes Contributing to the Growth of Distance Education

Although technological improvements have made the expansion of distance education possible, technology is not the only factor driving the interest in distance learning. Broader changes in the environment of higher education are also at work, including the following.

1. *The increased requirements for higher education for career advancement.* The growing complexity of the environment of most occupations in today's society, as well as the increased complexity of the occupations themselves, requires higher education to understand societal change, to stay abreast of one's competition, and to advance in one's occupation or profession. Today, distance delivery methods provide access to higher education for nontraditional learners who live beyond commuting distance of a campus.

2. *The demand for flexible scheduling by potential students whose daily routines are complex and do not mesh with the rhythm of the traditional educational day.* Increasingly, students of traditional college age work 20 or more hours per week to finance their education. Older students often juggle full-time day jobs and child-rearing responsibilities that are not compatible with the traditional campus schedule. Distance learning methods offer busy students opportunities to meet their educational objectives as well as their work and familial responsibilities.

3. *The growing market for personal fulfillment courses driven by increased personal income in some sectors of society.* Increasing affluence and longevity and a heightened concern for one's quality of life seem to be coupled with a growing consumer demand for opportunities to pursue special interests such as health and wellness, personal finance, and crafts and hobbies. The falling prices of personal computers and increasingly available access to Internet connections make it possible for higher education institutions to use distance programs to supply these opportunities to consumers located in areas previously inaccessible geographically.

4. *The general shift in the public's attitude from one that views education as a youthful pursuit to one that values lifelong learning.* Higher education in the past tended to be viewed in some (unenlightened) circles as a pursuit of young adults seeking entry to prestigious and well-paying employment. It is now well recognized that continuing intellectual engagement protects the mind—and possibly the body—from some of the ravages of aging. Distance learning makes it possible to continue one's intellectual life throughout adulthood in the convenience of one's home without the burden of travel.

5. *The growing requirement in many professions that members take additional coursework every year or two for license renewal.* Law, teaching, social work, and nursing are but a few examples. Distance education eliminates commuting time and is therefore especially attractive to busy professionals.

6. *The emphasis that many employers today place on specific competencies, rather than degrees, in their hiring.* Distance learning has the potential to pool students from a large geographic area, thereby enabling cost-effective instruction targeted to specific needs. Moreover, training can be delivered electronically directly to the job site.

7. *The shift by educators from teacher-centered education to student-centered learning.* Some forms of distance learning are compatible with this movement. For example, Web-based courses can build in greater choice for learners than can ITV or traditional classroom instruction.

8. *The increasing awareness among educators that students vary greatly in their learning styles.* The various modes of distance education offer alternative ways of learning that can help level the playing field for those students whose learning styles are not compatible with the traditional classroom.

9. *The need for greater flexibility in providing educational access to students with disabilities.* Distance education can reduce barriers of mobility and transportation. It can provide alternative formats, for example, Web-based instruction for students who are hearing impaired. (We will have more to say about this in Chapter 7.)

10. *The variation in students' willingness to participate in class.* Some students are reluctant to participate in discussions in the traditional classroom or to respond orally to instructors' questions because of their cultural background, family upbringing, or personal temperament, among other reasons. Distance education relies less on oral skills and more on written interaction, for example, in Web-based discussion groups and chat rooms. Not surprisingly, we have seen instances in which low-participating students in traditional classrooms became active participants in Web-based discussions.

11. *The increased pressure on public institutions of higher learning from legislatures and governors to develop cost-effective models of collaboration with other institutions of higher education.* Distance education holds much potential for institutions to concentrate their resources on developing certain strengths while enabling their students to take advantage of other collaborating institutions' special areas of expertise, regardless of their physical location.

Taken together, these factors have generated a great deal of interest and investment in distance education by institutions of higher learning. Indeed, distance education has come into the mainstream of higher education and is available from a wide spectrum of institutions. Distance education clearly no longer is a fringe activity or something engaged in only by those institutions whose missions include outreach to rural areas.

The Impact of Distance Education on Traditional Instruction

Distance education is changing traditional classroom instruction itself. Competition among institutions to respond to learning on demand and new developments in digital technology have led many institutions to revise the ways in which they offer traditional classroom courses. Increasingly, these courses incorporate Internet components such as Web sites, e-mail, threaded discussions, chat rooms, and listservs (see Chapter 5). These supplemented classroom-based courses are called *Web-enhanced* courses, as distinct from *Web-based* courses, in which the majority of the interaction occurs electronically. Many of these enhancements can be effected asynchronously, providing students with both convenient access and greater schedule flexibility.

These enhancements also give students more ability to direct their own learning, in that the Web-related features afford students considerable choice in selecting what discussions to pursue, what resources to seek out, and what topics to investigate more deeply. In this way, distance education is facilitating the shift from teacher-centered to student-centered learning, from passive to active and participatory learning. Similarly, many aspects of distance education are conducive to teamwork and collaboration among students at a time when employers are also placing greater emphasis on teamwork and collaboration.

The development of software packages such as WebCT and Blackboard,[1] which set up templates for a variety of Web-based course features, has made it easier for faculty with little background in online instruction to enter the realm of distance education.

In addition to its effects on classroom instruction, distance education is affecting higher learning institutions in several other ways. First, it is stimulating greater competition among educational institutions. Distance education is challenging geographic and jurisdictional boundaries, both within countries and globally. Institutions can expand their enrollments by serving student populations far beyond their traditional home territories. Private, for-profit institutions such as the University of Phoenix have emerged on the scene, garnering substantial enrollments of students traditionally served by not-for-profit educational institutions. Some public institutions, such as UCLA, are also aggressively marketing distance courses to the entire country and beyond. Other institutions are being drawn into distance education defensively, viewing it as a way of preventing erosion of their enrollments.

Second, distance education is also stimulating cooperation among institutions of higher education. New consortia of higher learning institutions are being formed to deliver degree programs that draw on the strengths of member institutions, for example, the Western Governors' University. Proponents argue that distance education will help create a more rational and efficient deployment of the nation's educational resources by facilitating the sharing and exchange of individual institutions' specialized expertise. Universities and colleges will not be obliged to spread their resources across so many disciplines and specialties but will be able to focus them more in selected areas.

Third, distance education is forcing a reevaluation of certain aspects of traditional higher education that have been assumed to be effective but have not been empirically demonstrated to be so. Educators, administrators, and accrediting bodies have appropriately questioned the instructional effectiveness of each form of distance education and have used traditional higher education as the benchmark. But many of those who design evaluative studies of distance education correctly note the lack of empirical research on the educational outcomes of traditional instruction. Much educational research in the past has focused on inputs, not outcomes. This response has spurred new research on outcomes of both traditional and distance education, including studies that compare traditional and distance teaching of the same content by the same instructors. A number of studies (Biner, Dean, & Mellinger, 1994; Zirkin & Sumler, 1995) suggest comparability of educational results and student satisfaction for traditional and distance education.

Criticisms of Distance Education

Several objections are often raised concerning distance education, a frequent assertion being that distance learning lacks the richness of experience afforded in a classroom milieu of colearners. Some modes of distance education can be structured to facilitate student-student and student-instructor interaction in ways that can equal or exceed the amount of interaction in a traditional classroom. Although the vehicles for interaction may be different, they can be organized to provide an intense educational experience.

Others argue that institutions offering distance programs cannot provide sufficient supports and resources to students. We address this concern more fully in Chapter 7 but note here some ways that supports can be provided. For ITV and satellite learning, many programs have found it essential to have local coordinators to facilitate students' experience at the distant sites. The coordinators sometimes serve several courses involving largely the same cohort of students, and they can also facilitate small group in-class activities. It is also important to have technicians available to help with the adjustment of electronic equipment. Students typically access learning resources through a combination of means: local campus and public libraries; electronic indexes, databases, and journals; resources on the World Wide Web; and mailed materials from the sponsoring college or university library. Some institutions' libraries have become especially attuned to the needs of distance learners and have established electronic reserves and other arrangements to support them (see, for example, the University of Minnesota Libraries Web site at www.lib.umn.edu/dist/). These are important concerns, and accrediting bodies look closely at library and other support services for distance learners.

A related criticism is that when done well, distance education involves costly expenditures that reduce or eliminate any cost advantage—extra staffing (site facilitators, technical support staff, faculty trainers) and investment in equipment (servers, software, high-speed transmission lines, electronic classrooms, etc.). This is true. The experience of many institutions is that a quality distance education program does not save money compared with traditional instruction, and, in some cases, it may be more costly. Distance education, however, can enhance an institution's ability to fulfill its outreach mission by enabling it to serve previously inaccessible audiences. Moreover, some of the tools developed for use in distance programs, such as course Web sites, can also enrich the institution's traditional classroom courses.

An additional criticism concerning costs is that distance education requires substantial initial investment in technology that may become obsolete. True, both hardware and software are constantly being improved (it is also true that for some items, costs are declining, not increasing). Computer equipment becomes outdated even more rapidly than transmission equipment. At some point, however, the institution needs to make the investment, or it will not be able to initiate its distance programs and may not stay competitive with institutions having a similar mission. An important consideration in selecting equipment is the likelihood that it will continue to be compatible with new systems.

Costs are involved also in training and supporting faculty providing distance education. Extra time is required of faculty, especially initially, to learn to use new course design principles, new teaching techniques, new software, and asynchronous modalities for communicating with students and student groups. Some of this may also require evening and weekend involvement—time that is no longer available for research or for keeping abreast of one's discipline. These additional demands on faculty time can be alleviated in part by providing institutional support in the form of orientation sessions, software training, mentoring arrangements, technical assistance in preparing teaching materials (electronic and otherwise), and, at least initially, reduced teaching loads. Faculty and staff development is essential to success in distance education.

Some see distance programs as a potential threat to their institution's reputation or as a possible threat to its accreditation. A number of studies, however, have found that the educational outcomes of distance education are comparable with those of traditional higher education (Biner et al., 1994; Zirkin & Sumler, 1995). Distance learning has gained recognition and respect from many quarters; indeed, some prestigious institutions now offer degree programs through distance education. Accrediting bodies are recognizing the advantages of distance education for fulfillment of institutional mission. As we explain in Chapter 11, many agencies are modifying or have already modified their accreditation requirements to encompass these new realities.

Not all higher learning institutions, however, will be attracted to distance education. Some will see their mission as providing a traditional, residential 2- or 4-year degree program to full-time, traditional college-age students. Even these institutions, however, are likely to use Web-enhanced instruction sooner or later. Other institutions, including some graduate institutions, do not perceive outreach to hitherto inaccessible audiences to be an important part of their mission and will be unlikely to develop distance degree programs. Some of these institutions, however, will nevertheless find it worthwhile, and even strategic, to offer certain courses in selected fields through distance education.

Conclusion

Distance education is not a new phenomenon, but changes in the larger society and the growth of new technologies for instructional delivery have increased the public's awareness of and demand for distance education so that it does appear to be a "new thing." These same societal and technological changes have altered the nature of higher education institutions and instruction itself. Although a number of criticisms have been leveled against distance education, it complements traditional classroom-based instruction, providing invaluable service to those students previously denied access to higher education because of geographic barriers or scheduling difficulties. At the same time, distance education methods show great promise in the areas of continuing professional education, personal enrichment, and lifelong learning.

$\underline{\text{Www}}_{\blacktriangleright}$ At our Sage Web site, www.sagepub.com/mehrotra

---

On our companion Web site are links to additional information about the history of distance education; links to current reports on trends in distance learning, including recent surveys; and a listing of journals related to distance education.

Note

1. When we refer to a commercial product, any such citation is by way of giving an example of a tool having a particular capability or feature. We do not intend to exclude similar products, nor are we offering an endorsement of any product.

References

Biner, P. M., Dean, R. S., & Mellinger, A. E. (1994). Factors underlying distance learner satisfaction with televised college-level courses. *American Journal of Distance Education, 8*(1), 60-71.

National Center for Education Statistics. (1999). *Distance education at post-secondary education institutions: 1997-98* (NCES 2000-013). Washington, DC: U.S. Department of Education.

Zirkin, B. G., & Sumler, D. E. (1995). Interactive or non-interactive? That is the question! An annotated bibliography. *Journal of Distance Education, 10*(1), 95-112.

2

Attracting Students to
Distance Learning

In this chapter, we provide some suggestions for attracting students to a distance education program, an obviously important concern if the endeavor is to be financially feasible. Thus, considerable thought needs to go into the institution's strategies for recruiting students to its distance programs (and to supporting them once they are enrolled—a topic discussed more fully in Chapter 7).

The strategies for attracting distance students need to be designed in relation to each of the other aspects of the program and should follow from them. A sound assessment of the need and demand for distance education will help identify the specific population(s) to be targeted by the program. The characteristics of the target population will, in turn, help shape the instructional design, which in turn should heavily influence the choice of the mode for delivering the instruction. Problems or new issues encountered at any phase can also impinge on

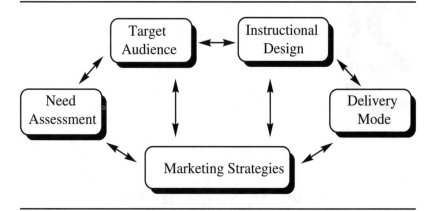

Figure 2.1. Marketing's Relation to Other Components of Distance Education Planning

earlier phases (Moore & Kearsley, 1996). Each phase has both a direct and an indirect relationship to the marketing strategies, as diagrammed in Figure 2.1.

How to Assess the Need and Demand for a Distance Program

Institutions with a history of outreach and extension are probably in a better position to gauge the probable need and demand for distance courses than those with no outreach history because they already have experience in offering traditional courses on evenings or weekends or at off-campus locations. These institutions, however, will also benefit from a careful assessment of need. There are a variety of techniques for measuring need, none of which is completely sufficient to be used alone. Among the more useful techniques for assessing need for distance education are surveys, secondary data analysis, community meetings, focus groups, and use of expert opinion. Employing two or more techniques and a comparison of the results can be helpful. To the extent that the findings converge to suggest a demand, the institution can have more confidence that a proposed distance program will be well subscribed. Witkin and Artschuld (1995) have written a useful guide for performing needs assessments.

Several pools of potential students can be queried by surveys: alumni; past and current students enrolled in courses offered on weekends and evenings and off-campus; professionals, such as nurses, teachers, and social workers (address lists can usually be obtained through the state unit handling licensing); and so on. The surveys can be helpful both for identifying the course topics and fields of greatest interest and for assessing prospective students' acceptance of the media for distance instruction. Even a moderately strong interest in distance learning indicated by a survey, however, should be viewed with caution. Some of those giving a positive response will not enroll when the realities of the specific class schedule and time commitment become known. In the case of degree programs, some prospects expressing interest may not meet the minimum admission qualifications for prerequisite courses or for prior academic performance. Surveys mailed to the general population are unlikely to yield useful information, but surveys of special groups, such as recent graduates and prospective employers, can be helpful.

These surveys should be designed in accordance with established procedures (see, for example, Rubin & Babbie, 2001) so that the information secured will be of sufficiently high quality to be trustworthy. First, the information needed should be carefully determined; the survey should then be limited to obtaining that information. The longer the survey instrument, the greater the risk of losing potential respondents. Among the items often included are questions ascertaining students' educational background and other demographic characteristics; their experience with distance education; their preferences for a learning modality; the distance they are willing to travel (important when delivery is by ITV or if online learning is to be supplemented with occasional in-person meetings); hours available for participation (important if live interaction is required); access to computers and libraries; and, of course, subjects and fields of greatest interest.

Analysis of data available from other sources—the Census Bureau, the state's department of education (e.g., high school graduation data), or a state's higher education coordinating body—can be used to better understand the potential markets in specific regions.

Because ITV-based instruction usually targets specific geographic locations, it can be advantageous to hold meetings with employers and others who have expert knowledge regarding the needs in that area for distance education. For example, before the University of Minnesota initiated a distance master of social work degree program, the program administrators held several meetings with prospective social service employers and officials of local educational institutions at each of the sites under consideration. These meetings indicated that sufficient demand and local support existed to proceed with the program. In some instances, it also may be possible to develop a contractual agreement with an employer or cluster of employers to provide distance instruction to a group of their employees. Institutions ranging from vocational-technical schools to universities offering graduate degrees have successfully used this approach, which also reduces the financial risk to the institution by guaranteeing an audience.

Community information meetings can be scheduled at local educational institutions or libraries to discuss possible distance programming with prospective students, parents, employers, and other interested parties; the same meetings allow the institution to collect community input and gauge reaction to the proposed program. If the meetings are well publicized in advance, they can provide helpful feedback on the extent of demand for various courses and programs. A roster of those attending one of these forums can become the nucleus of a list of contacts for follow-up marketing once the programs are established.

An incremental approach may be a good strategy for a college or university seeking to start a distance education program. Before initiating a complete distance degree program, it is wise for the institution first to offer a few distance courses. This affords an opportunity to measure students' response to distance education, to obtain a better sense of the potential market, and to provide the institution and participating faculty members with valuable experience in distance instruction. These pioneering faculty members often later become informal consultants to faculty participating in distance programs.

One or several groups of students who enrolled in these initial distance courses can be convened into focus groups to secure specific suggestions for improving the courses. Krueger (1994) describes ways to maximize the quality of the feedback from focus groups. In the meantime, those students who have completed distance courses often help create additional interest in distance offerings through their conversations with coworkers and friends.

In short, initially delivering just a few courses enables the institution to experiment with distance education without having to commit the resources needed to support an entire program, thus reducing the financial risk. After gaining some experience with distance courses, the institution may be ready to commit to offering a full distance degree program.

Target Audience

What individuals is the distance program trying to reach? Part-time learners? Older learners? People seeking improved job skills, general education, specialized certificates or graduate degrees, or courses for personal fulfillment? Learners who live or work at considerable geographic distance? Persons with special needs or disabilities? Resident students (who may want the more flexible schedule of distance education or a more learner-driven approach to instruction)?

Distance courses have been successfully targeted to each of the aforementioned audiences, and others in addition. The characteristics and preferences of each category of potential users vary somewhat, however, which should be taken into account in designing the instruction and developing its marketing strategy. Older learners may respond better to videotapes and ITV instruction than do younger learners, who tend to have more experience with computers and the Web. People with busy schedules are likely to respond better to asynchronous learning than do those who have more time available. Likewise, ITV may not be feasible for learners whose dispersal across a large geographic distance or rugged terrain may preclude travel to a receiving site or where weather conditions frequently make travel unsafe. Learners also vary in their access to computers and to the high-speed connections required for some types of computer-based instruction, as noted in Chapter 5. This may become less of a problem as the cost of computers continues to decline, as the use of personal computers becomes increasingly commonplace, as the infrastructure for high-speed connections continues to be extended, and as community libraries expand public access to the Web, thereby increasing access for those who cannot afford computers. There is much concern about the "digital divide" in today's society. Expanding community libraries' public Internet facilities is one means of addressing this problem.

Distance learning attracts students who also differ somewhat from the general student population. For example, Elliott, Ambrosia, and Case (1999) characterize their community college's distance learners as follows:

> Our most successful distance learning students share several key characteristics:
>
> > *Goal oriented.* Many want specific job-related courses and all expect to get their money's worth from college.
> >
> > *Highly motivated.* They are self-directed learners with good reading and time management skills, and they are willing to work independently.
> >
> > *Focused learners.* They are learners who often enroll for the pure joy of learning.
> >
> > *Risk-takers.* They are willing to try new ways of learning.
> >
> > *Thrive when guided and encouraged by their instructors.* They do best when they are integrated into the institution's social and support structures and given personal mentoring. (p. 67)

The last point also highlights the importance to distance learning of support services and social integration, topics we address in Chapters 7 and 8. Elliott and coauthors go on to note that these characteristics fit well with distance learning, which, more than traditional instruction, requires students to manage their own learning process, to be more assertive, and to participate actively in the instructional process.

Instructional Design and Mode of Delivery

Chapters 3 and 4 will address principles of instructional design that should be incorporated into the planning of distance learning, while Chapters 5 and 6 will outline considerations involved in selecting the mode of delivery of distance learning. Throughout this book, we stress that the selection of the mode of delivery should follow from the instructional design, not vice versa. With these ideas in mind, we can now turn to marketing strategies that can be used in developing distance education.

Strategies for Marketing
Distance Courses and Programs

A basic marketing principle is to know the comparative advantages and disadvantages of the product. Distance education is attractive for learners because it reduces barriers of both geography and schedule and can be responsive to learners with special needs. It opens up access to learning to large numbers of persons who previously could not enroll because they lived too far away, because their work or family schedules did not allow them to take courses at traditional times and locations, or because they had special needs that prevented their enrollment on campus. Thus, the *flexibility* of distance education is a major advantage.

A second advantage is the opportunity that distance education provides to learn from classmates from *different backgrounds and locales.* For example, ITV courses can help urban-based professionals better understand the challenges facing their rural counterparts, and vice versa. Web-based courses, on the other hand, can involve students from many geographic areas and sometimes from several countries.

A third advantage is that some forms of distance education, such as Web-based or Web-enhanced courses, permit learning to be *student driven* rather than instructor driven. This feature of distance education appeals to many adult learners and busy professionals and should be stressed in promotional materials.

A fourth advantage is *faculty resources.* Faculty from different college campuses are sometimes coinstructors of the same course. This can provide greater breadth and depth than instruction by one faculty member alone. For example, in the fall of 2000, six professors from six Southern universities began teaching an advanced Latin course via the Internet (Young, 2000a).

All these advantages can be built into the themes used to market distance education, with special emphasis placed on the convenience, flexibility, and greater opportunity to direct one's own learning. Many potential distance learners, however, have not previously taken anything other than traditional classroom courses, and some may be uneasy about courses delivered electronically or through other media. Moreover, many prospective students (and some faculty) are skeptical that distance education can be of as high a quality as traditional classroom education, or that even if it is of high quality, it may not be valued highly by prospective employers. These are important questions that need to be fully explored with prospective students. On the one hand, it is important to communicate to prospective students that there is ample evidence that distance education is equivalent to traditional education. Distance education is not the same as traditional education, but each modality has certain advantages and disadvantages (as well as a lot in common). The quality and educational outcomes of distance education have been found in many studies to be equivalent, *when there has been sound educational design.* The empirical findings regarding the equivalence of outcomes of distance learning are similar and encouraging across a wide array of disciplines and instructional technologies (Russell, 1999). On the other hand, the research designs used in some studies of distance learning have not been adequate to permit definitive conclusions about equivalence (Phipps & Merisotis, 1999). It is important to be honest with prospective students—to say that the research done to date is generally encouraging, that it suggests that distance learning has approximately equivalent outcomes in many subjects, and also that more comprehensive studies are still needed.

It may assist marketing efforts to emphasize that some of the leading institutions in the United States and overseas offer distance education programs (Carr, 2000) and to note that employers, too, appreciate the flexibility that distance education provides to employees. In addition, marketers may point out that distance and traditional education technologies are converging—distance technologies are increasingly also being used in resident instruction. For example, Northwestern University recently announced plans to wire all dormitory rooms on campus to enable students to use computers in their rooms to call up a variety of video-based instructional materials (Young, 2000b). More and more resident courses are incorporating Web-based components, even when all the students enrolled are resident students. Tutoring is also sometimes delivered electronically.

Prospective students need to be informed of the variety of means available to interact with the instructor and with other learners and to know that they will receive prompt feedback from the instructor on the assignments they submit. Prospective students should also be informed that initiative will be required on their part because distance education is more learner directed than is traditional learning. An upfront discussion of expectations of students is also an important part of the strategy for ensuring that distance learning programs attract learners who have a high probability of success.

Although administrators and faculty can and should draw from the national (and international) literature in promoting their institution's distance education programs, they most certainly should undertake studies at their own institutions to compare learning outcomes and student satisfaction with traditional and distance courses and curricula and to identify the characteristics of those who enroll and those who complete distance courses and programs. Institutions should also convene focus groups (see earlier discussion) of distance students to receive feedback on the program. The results from these studies will be useful for marketing as well as for program improvement.

Specific Ideas for Promoting and Marketing Distance Programs

A variety of means are available to attract distance students. To achieve the maximum impact for marketing, the recruitment strategy should be developed in cooperation with the office of admissions and the office that handles the institution's publicity and external relations. Here are some specific ideas to consider incorporating into the marketing plan:

1. Create a Web page specifically on the distance programs:

   a. Provide a description of the program, the career opportunities to which it can lead, and admission requirements; a description of how distance learning works; and a description of the support services available to learners, such as financial aid, libraries, advising, career services, and so on. (See also the discussion of support services in Chapter 7.)

   b. Include the schedule of distance courses and also detailed course descriptions (and possibly even syllabi).

c. Link the Web page to other frequently visited pages on the institution's Web site, such as descriptions of the degree and certificate
programs, the college catalogue, the schedule of classes, and
information about faculty.

d. Consider contracting with one or more of the commercial firms
that have set up Web-based and/or print directories to list the
institution and Web site along with other institutions offering
courses through distance education, such as the *Guide to Distance
Learning Programs* (2000).

e. Post a brief sample lesson from a course on the Web site to give
students a better idea of how a Web-based or Web-enhanced session works. If the course uses streaming video, then a brief sample of a lecture using streaming video could be put on the Web
site. (Likewise, for courses based on videotapes or compact discs
[CDs], a minilecture could be included on a promotional videotape or CD mailed out to prospective students.) This helps students experience how the program works, promotes active learning, provides feedback at the end of each module, and allows
students to interact with others.

f. Include on the Web site a Frequently Asked Questions (FAQ)
page, and update it frequently on the basis of experience and
comments from students. A good example of a FAQ page is the
one operated by OnlineLearning.net (www.onlinelearning.net/
StudentServices/CourseManagers/index.cfm?s=920.50101602p.
110b107d20).

g. Include a link to the library's Web site that explains the services
available to distance learners, the interlibrary loan system, and (if
available) the library's electronic reserve system. For example,
see the University of Minnesota site (www.lib.umn.edu/dist/).

h. On the Web site and in other publicity materials, provide a toll-
free number that enables prospective students to connect with the
administrative coordinator, with course instructors, and with
other campus offices to get questions answered.

2. Establish a listserv that will provide announcements of new distance
courses and other notices automatically to those who have subscribed
to it. Then build in an opportunity on the Web site for interested persons to subscribe to the listserv. For an example of an active listserv

sponsored by UCLA and other institutions, send an e-mail to OnlineLearning.net (updates2000@onlinelearning.net).

3. Also use traditional media, such as press releases, newspaper advertisements, radio and television advertisements, and brochures and flyers, for announcing new courses and programs and publicizing increases in enrollments and other developments.

   a. Place stories and announcements in catalogs and bulletins, alumni publications, and newsletters.

   b. Include in the above some short descriptions of, and quotations from, individual students or graduates who have taken distance courses and degree programs (with their permission, of course). Prospective students will find firsthand accounts of students' experiences with distance learning interesting and helpful.

4. Seek out alumni of distance programs willing to be contacted individually about their distance learning experiences by prospective distance students. This personal contact will help demystify the learning process.

5. Publicize distance education courses to resident students as well as to current and prospective distance students. Many resident students are interested in trying a distance course. In some distance courses, a third or more of the students may be resident students. Their enrollment obviously helps support distance education financially, and (for ITV) it helps create for viewers a setting that is more like a traditional classroom by providing an audience that is in the same room as the instructor. (In addition, many ITV instructors prefer to have a live audience in front of them rather than to speak only to a camera.) In addition, some resident students will respond to an opportunity to take a course that is Web based because it is more student driven and enables more flexible use of time.

6. For ITV-based instruction, consider a rotational plan, whereby a distance program is delivered to a particular community for 2 to 4 years and then moves on to another community. Some graduate professional programs have used this strategy to great advantage, while also fulfilling the expectations for their institutions to reach out more to rural areas. For example, both Michigan State University and California State University at Long Beach have rotated the distance versions of their master of social work degree programs to several communities.

7. Before taking a distance education program into a community, contact key employers in that area to gain their advice on local needs and to secure their support in publicizing the program. Sometimes, employers will also contribute toward employees' tuition costs. Encourage prospective students to check with employers about possible tuition subsidies.

8. Earlier, we suggested using community meetings to help gauge demand for distance programming. Once a decision has been made to go ahead with distance courses or programs, another set of community meetings can be scheduled to help market the new distance learning opportunities. Contacting the local media in advance about such meetings can add to the number of prospects. In conducting the meetings, be forthright both about the equivalence of, and the differences between, distance and traditional education. This will help attract those most able to benefit from distance programs.

9. Wherever possible, include in the information sessions a demonstration of the technology to be used. For example, demonstrate an ITV hookup with participants on the home campus, a course Web site or a chat room, an electronic reserve system, and so on. This helps prospective students better understand the similarities to and differences from the education they have previously received.

10. Specify the equipment that students will need to purchase or access, such as computers. Check in advance the availability to students of local public facilities, such as computers and Internet access in local educational institutions or libraries. Include minimum hardware and software requirements on the Web page.

11. Reassure prospective students of the supports available to distance learners—financial aid, advising, library supports, tutoring, career services, site coordinators, multiple ways of communicating with faculty and staff (toll-free line, e-mail, fax, etc.), timeliness of instructors' responses, and so on. (See Chapter 7 for a more detailed discussion concerning support services for distance learners.)

12. Clarify accreditation concerns to prospective students, regarding both the general accreditation status of the institution and the accreditation specific to certain disciplines and professions. (See Chapter 11 for a discussion of these concerns.)

13. If a distance degree program is offered in cooperation with a local educational institution, try to arrange publicity about the program through that institution's media and events, for example, its com-

mencement ceremony. Sometimes, the local institution finds it advantageous to include the graduating distance cohort in its own commencement ceremonies. (This also may increase convenience for students' families and friends living in that area.) The local institution gains recognition as a facilitator of wider educational opportunities for the local community, and the degree-granting institution gains an opportunity to further publicize its distance program and the types of learners it serves.

14. Assure degree- or certificate-seeking students about the institution's commitment to seeing them all the way through the degree or certificate program, including that portion of the program to be offered at a distance. Then *honor* the commitment, so that students are not abandoned if the distance program has lower enrollments than projected. In making such a commitment, it is sometimes necessary for the institution's financial self-protection to state up front at the information sessions that the program will not be initiated unless there is a certain minimum number of admissions.

Conclusion

Attracting students to distance education requires coordination of the marketing strategies with the assessment of the need for distance education, identification of the target audience, instructional design, and selection of the mode of instructional delivery. By combining some of the strategies noted previously with knowledge of community needs and of the institution's linkages to the community, a well-designed distance education program should be able to attract a number of qualified applicants. Once they are enrolled, the next challenge is to provide adequate support for their learning. This is the subject of Chapter 7.

WWw ▸ At our Sage Web site, www.sagepub.com/mehrotra

Visit our Sage Publications Web site to take a marketing tour—follow the links to see how schools already involved in distance education market their programs. Also included are additional references to studies on characteristics and preferences of distance learners.

References

Carr, S. (2000, October 6). Oxford, Princeton, Stanford, and Yale plan distance-education venture. *Chronicle of Higher Education, 47*(6), A48.

Elliott, B., Ambrosia, A., & Case, P. (1999). A systems approach to asynchronous distance learning. In M. Boaz, B. Elliott, D. Foshee, D. Hardy, C. Jarmon, & D. Olcott Jr. (Eds.), *Teaching at a distance: A handbook for instructors* (Chap. 6). Mission Viejo, CA: League for Innovation in the Community College and Archipelago Productions.

Guide to distance learning programs. (2000). Lawrenceville, NJ: Peterson's, Thomson Learning in cooperation with University Continuing Education Association.

Krueger, R. (1994). *Focus groups: A practical guide for applied research* (2nd ed.). Thousand Oaks, CA: Sage.

Moore, M. G., & Kearsley, G. (1996). *Distance education: A systems view.* Belmont, CA: Wadsworth.

Phipps, R., & Merisotis, J. (1999). *What's the difference? A review of contemporary research on the effectiveness of distance learning in higher education.* Washington, DC: Institute for Higher Education Policy.

Rubin, A., & Babbie, E. R. (2001). *Research methods for social work* (4th ed.). Belmont, CA: Wadsworth.

Russell, T. L. (1999). *The "no significant difference" phenomenon as reported in 355 research reports, summaries and papers.* Raleigh: North Carolina State University Office of Instructional Telecommunications.

Witkin, B. R., & Artschuld, J. W. (1995). *Planning and conducting a needs assessment: A practical guide.* Thousand Oaks, CA: Sage.

Young, J. R. (2000a, July 7). Moving the seminar table to the computer screen. *Chronicle of Higher Education, 46*(44), A33.

Young, J. R. (2000b, September 8). Northwestern U. wires its dormitories for online video instruction. *Chronicle of Higher Education, 47*(2), A60.

3

Good Practices
in Distance Education

How to Promote
Student Learning and Development

Although we may use different strategies to promote learning in distance education courses, learning theories and principles that have been found successful in the traditional classroom remain constant regardless of the delivery mechanism. Good practices in undergraduate education outlined by Chickering and Gamson (1991) are, therefore, as applicable to distance learning as to the traditional classroom. The resources made available by technological advances offer particular promise for implementing good practices, for helping

29

students develop effective communication skills, for facilitating collaboration among the students, and for engaging them in active learning. The instructors in distance education courses, however, need to use creative approaches to realize the potential of technology to foster student learning. In this chapter, we offer tips that readers may find useful in teaching their students at a distance. What we present for each practice should not be viewed as a comprehensive compendium. Instead, our suggestions should be viewed as a sample of approaches that may serve as a starting point and stimulate readers to create their own strategies. It is important to emphasize that the strategies developed should match the course content and the learning outcomes that the students are expected to achieve.

Although some courses require continual interaction between the instructor and the students, there are others for which occasional contact may be adequate. Furthermore, within the same course, there may be selected topics or competencies for which student-student interaction and/or student-instructor interaction may be essential and other topics for which such interaction may not be as necessary.

Before launching our discussion on good practices, it is important to emphasize that instructors need to be careful in managing their time. Although time management is important in all courses, this skill is especially relevant in designing new courses and making them available to students at a distance. Even when an instructor has taught a course on campus, adapting it for a distance learning mode requires careful thought and planning—at least one or two semesters before offering the course. This means that both instructor and institution need to allocate the required time for developing a course syllabus, designing assignments, creating assessment procedures, and securing copyright clearances. As a part of creating the course design, instructors also need to think about the time that they plan to devote to teaching the course. On the basis of our experience with teaching such courses, the time commitment is substantial even for 20 students. Thus, although the practices we present in this chapter have been found effective in enhancing student learning, which of them are used and to what extent will depend on the design of the course, the outcomes expected of students, the number of students in the course, and the time instructors are able to devote.

The Good Practices

Good Practice 1: Encourage faculty-student contact.

Frequent student-faculty contact is the most important focus in student motivation and involvement. Faculty concern helps students get through rough times and keep on working. Knowing a few faculty members well enhances students' intellectual commitment and encourages them to think about their own values and plans. (Chickering & Gamson, 1991, pp. 14-15)

Instructors in distance education courses can use available technology to maintain contact with their students. Below are some tips readers may find useful.

1. *Encourage students to contact you via e-mail with their questions, and respond promptly to the messages you receive.* Having e-mail access to the instructor promotes communication and allows many shy students to ask their instructor questions that they may not have asked in front of other members of the class. Students use e-mail to converse with the instructor regarding the course objectives, readings, assignments, and other aspects of the class. They appreciate receiving a prompt response from the instructor and feel encouraged to ask additional questions as the need arises. In addition to responding to student questions, instructors also use e-mail to provide them with individualized feedback on their papers, assignments, quizzes, and exams. Such communication is effective because it is more personalized, protected, and convenient than the more intimidating demands of face-to-face interaction. Of course, this implies that the instructors need to pay special attention to the language, tone, and style they use in e-mail communication with their students. Encouraging notes from instructors make a difference for the students, especially when they feel isolated in small communities away from the college campus.

2. *Provide students with a toll-free telephone number to contact you.* Although e-mail provides an effective vehicle for sustained contact between faculty and students, there are times when learners need to have

an oral conversation with the instructor. Providing all students with a toll-free number sends a clear message about the instructor's availability to talk with them in times of need, gives students an opportunity to seek clarification regarding an assignment or an examination, and helps them move forward when they are having difficulty with some material in the course. It has been our experience that students do not make unnecessary use of the telephone, calling only when a problem or an issue requires immediate resolution.

3. *Synthesize the key points from the discussion created by the questions, case studies, or other stimuli you had provided.* Many instructors use technology to promote discussion among the participants in distance learning by providing them with case studies, field projects, study questions, quizzes, or other stimuli. Teachers monitor the group discussion, examine the themes that surface, and track who participates and who does not. On the basis of their observations, instructors can then post responses to frequently asked questions. We have found this approach quite effective when a number of students are asking the same questions or when clarification or additional information is needed regarding the topic under discussion. Students also appreciate the teacher bringing closure to a discussion by offering a synthesis of what was presented, answering questions they have raised, interpreting the discussion, and connecting it with the next unit(s) of the course. Such participation as a discussion facilitator and synthesizer keeps the instructor apprised of the students' experience of the course, which concepts or principles they find difficult, how they are learning from each other, and what progress they are making toward achieving the expected course outcomes. Knowing that their instructor is following the discussion not only affects the quality of students' contribution but also keeps them aware of their contact with the instructor. This awareness keeps them motivated and actively engaged and promotes a sense of being connected with each other and the instructor. An online or ITV discussion often brings out points that the instructor may not have planned to introduce, just as happens in a traditional on-campus classroom. In addition, it allows the instructors to develop an understanding of their students, their background, their interests, and sometimes their work environment.

Good Practice 2: Develop reciprocity and cooperation among students.

Learning is enhanced when it is more like a team effort than a solo race. Good learning, like good work, is collaborative and social, not competitive and isolated. Working with others increases involvement in learning. Sharing one's ideas and responding to others improves thinking and deepens understanding. (Chickering & Gamson, 1991, pp. 16-17)

Given the isolation experienced by many distance education students, and recognizing the value of collaboration and teamwork in enhancing learning, we offer the following suggestions to promote reciprocity and cooperation among students.

1. *Begin the class by inviting the students to introduce themselves.* This introduction can be made via Internet conference, chat room, or ITV and can include information about students' year in college, their place of current residence, their reasons for taking the course, their prior experience with distance learning, and their work setting. The instructor can participate in this process either by first introducing himself or herself or by providing a summary of the characteristics of the members of the class. Students appreciate learning about each other and the instructor. Our experience indicates that this practice helps develop collegiality in the course and promotes the development of networking relationships among the students. Having background information on those enrolled in the course allows the students to (a) identify their classmates with similar interests and backgrounds, (b) design and carry out collaborative projects, (c) exchange ideas about the material being covered in the course, and (d) respond to each other's questions as they arise. At the same time, each student's right to privacy and confidentiality must be respected; this may require obtaining written permission from the students before the introductions session occurs.

2. *Make a class list available to all the students enrolled in the course.* This list may include both e-mail and postal addresses. Students find this information helpful because it allows them to establish contact

with classmates who live nearby and/or share common interests. If the program includes some on-site meetings, this information also facilitates forming car pools, which contribute toward the goal of collaborative learning. Note again the importance of securing participants' permission before making such lists available—students should not feel pressured into providing information.

3. *Encourage teams of students to enroll in the course.* The master of education program provided by The College of St. Scholastica via distance learning for K-12 teachers provides students an incentive to form study teams by allowing them to submit their applications in one envelope and charging a single application fee regardless of team size. Experience indicates that members of the study teams often share their reactions to readings in their courses, undertake collaborative projects, travel together for on-site meetings, and support each other in many ways. This strategy not only creates communities of learners but also leads to high rates of retention and graduation.

4. *Provide opportunities for on-site activities to complement distance learning.* The likelihood of increased reciprocity and cooperation among students is often enhanced through face-to-face interaction in on-site activities. When students from different parts of a broad regional area enroll in a distance education program, an on-site orientation introduces them to the program as a whole, communicates the instructor and program expectations, engages them in discussing the readings that had been sent to them in advance, and promotes the development of networking relationships. An on-site session scheduled later in a course or program provides students an opportunity to present their research, solicit suggestions for further research, and review the progress that they have made with regard to the expected outcomes of the program as a whole.

5. *Involve students in sharing with each other their reactions to what they are learning.* We have already noted the effectiveness of students' participation in discussing the weekly topic as a means of sustaining their contact with the instructor. When the students present their viewpoints in the conference area of an online course or in the discussion session of an ITV course, they get to know each other and begin to form relationships that continue long after they have completed the course

or the program. One of our colleagues reports that some of the participants in her distance education course often call each other to discuss their work-related situations.

6. *Create opportunities for learning in pairs.* Research and experience show that working and studying in pairs can facilitate learning. This approach is especially useful in distance courses when students do not have the opportunity to interact with one another on a regular basis before, during, and after the in-class meetings. Instructors in distance learning courses may form dyads in which students ask and answer questions on commonly read books, journal articles, or other material that they can summarize later in an assigned reaction paper.

Good Practice 3: Use active learning techniques.

Learning is not a spectator sport. Students do not learn much just sitting in classes listening to teachers, memorizing prepackaged assignments, and spitting out answers. They must talk about what they are learning, write reflectively about it, relate it to past experiences, and apply it to their daily lives. They must make what they learn part of themselves. (Chickering & Gamson, 1991, pp. 17-18)

As indicated above, active learning involves providing opportunities for students to talk, listen, write, read, and reflect on the content, ideas, issues, and concerns of the course they are taking via distance learning. These elements involve cognitive activities that allow students to clarify questions, consolidate information, and appropriate new knowledge. These activities, however, need to be well structured and guided by instructors: Teachers serve not only as sources of disciplinary expertise but also as facilitators of learning. The expanding world of computers, interactive videos, and telecommunications can help instructors create instructional resources that engage their students in active learning. In this section, we present examples of strategies to promote students' engagement in learning.

1. *Create assignments that engage students in learning by doing.* A variety of methods practiced in on-campus courses can be adapted to promote active learning in distance education courses. Students may be given an assignment that requires them to use the Internet to gather

information not available in the library. Working on this type of assignment allows them to (a) learn how to find information on a given topic; (b) become aware of the differences in the quality of what is available; (c) realize that some of these articles have not received the level of scrutiny that is given to manuscripts accepted for publication; (d) develop the criteria they will use to discriminate between poor- and high-quality material; and (e) synthesize the findings from their search and present them in a systematic manner. Another strategy is to design data analysis exercises that students can complete by using instructor-provided data or a database available via the Internet. Although all students appreciate clearly structured learning assignments and schedules, this is especially true for students working at a distance. In creating the exercises aimed at engaging students in data analysis, it is critical that they receive detailed information on the intended learning objectives, the database to be used and how it is accessed, what analyses need to be performed, and how the results are to be reported. One of us employs this approach in an introductory statistics distance course taught with videotaped presentations. These assignments, interspersed throughout the course, provide students with problems of varying difficulty level. To help students check the accuracy of their work, the study package also includes answers to the analyses. When they have questions related to these assignments, they contact the instructor by toll-free telephone or e-mail.

As another variation of this assignment, the instructor may ask students to collect data to be analyzed using the techniques they have learned in the course to answer a list of questions. In one of our courses, students are required to design a questionnaire to test their hypotheses, administer it to collect the needed data, conduct data analysis, and prepare a research report. We provide written comments on various parts of the students' work, which leads to highly beneficial discussions regarding their experience with the assignment and its implications.

Many courses and programs involve more than lectures and discussions. Laboratories are a standard part of most science courses: Students learn science by doing science, often with expensive equipment or potentially dangerous substances that must be handled in controlled environments. Professional programs in the health fields require clinical experiences—opportunities for students to learn by doing under the guidance of a licensed professional in a hospital, clinic, or similar setting. These are but two examples.

Distance programs or courses incorporating labs, clinical experiences, and similar internships have special, although not insurmountable, challenges. For example, simple laboratory exercises for introductory or liberal arts science courses often can be constructed using everyday materials found around the house or readily available at hardware, grocery, and drugstores. Students can be led through the exercises with videos, Web pages, and printed manuals. As long as the materials can be used and disposed of safely, this approach may be quite successful. Extensive, detailed instructions and safety warnings must be provided. (Potential liability issues should be discussed with the institution's legal counsel.) If the main purpose of the laboratory exercise is the development of observational skills, data analysis, and problem-solving based on real data rather than on development of manipulative skills, a videotape, CD, or streaming video clip of the experiment could be created for students. Indeed, having the ability to repeatedly view the action "up close and personal" may actually be superior to having students perform the experiment poorly once or twice.

Clinical experience and sophisticated labs require students to gather at a particular site. The number of sessions, and hence the travel required of students, can be reduced with careful organization: A number of exercises can be scheduled within a half-day or full-day meeting, or it might be possible to create a single exercise integrating elements from several lessons. Alternatively, the necessary meetings could form the basis of a residential experience at the conclusion of the course. A third option is to make arrangements with another institution for providing the clinical or laboratory experience. As we said, incorporating labs or clinical experience into a distance education course or program can be challenging, so whether these course elements are necessary should be carefully considered.

2. *Design assignments that involve time-delayed exchange of ideas between two or more students.* In a number of distance courses in psychology and education, we ask students to read published articles, prepare critiques, and share their drafts with a classmate for peer review. This allows them to discuss what they have written, obtain constructive feedback, reflect on the issues raised during discussion, and incorporate significant changes in the critiques they have prepared. These cognitive activities occur within student-formed learning pairs. Students fax or mail their assignments to the study partner, exchange detailed

written comments, and then discuss by telephone the feedback they have received. When they submit the assignment to the instructor, students include both the preliminary draft, the final copy of the critique, and the reflection on what they experienced and learned in completing various phases of this project. Developing and assessing this assignment require the instructors to provide individualized feedback and to create the specific guidelines and structures that students need to have a good learning experience, but we have found that this instructional strategy incorporates the key elements of active learning—talking and listening, reading, writing, and reflecting on the experiences.

3. *Invite students to give a demonstration of a skill they have learned.* Student learning outcomes in many courses include acquisition of new skills. Examples include these: (a) A social work course requires that the students develop skills in conducting interviews with clients representing diverse backgrounds; (b) a psychology course includes administering an individual intelligence test (such as Stanford-Binet or Wechsler Intelligence Scale) to a 7-year-old student who is having difficulty in school; and (c) a chemistry course includes analyzing a given sample. Whether students are enrolled in on-campus courses or in distance learning programs, performing these tasks allows them to apply what they have learned, engages them in active learning, and prepares them for the world of work. With innovative use of television (live and recorded), telephone line-based teleconferencing, and computer-aided communications, these skill-based courses bring students and professors together despite their physical separation. In a social work course, one of us uses television to monitor students when they are conducting interviews at two sites. A similar approach can be employed when students are conducting analysis in the chemistry laboratory or administering an intelligence test in a remote location. (An on-site assistant supervisor may be needed, as in the case of laboratory work.) The individualized feedback and direction that students receive from the instructor in these cases significantly enhance the quality of the distance learning experience.

Good Practice 4: Give prompt feedback.

Knowing what you know and don't know focuses learning. Students need appropriate feedback on performance to benefit from courses.

When getting started, students need help in assessing existing knowledge and competence. In classes, students need frequent opportunities to perform and receive suggestions for improvement. At various points during college, and at the end, students need chances to reflect on what they have learned, what they still need to know, and how to assess themselves. (Chickering & Gamson, 1991, pp. 18-19)

Because many distance learning students experience limited face-to-face contact, they appreciate receiving timely, frequent, and helpful feedback regarding their progress toward the goals and objectives of the course. They hope to have their work treated with respect, to receive an explanation and justification given for the grade awarded, and to receive a clear explanation of how they could improve. They rightly expect that the feedback will have a helpful attitude or tone and will provide them appropriate reassurance about their abilities. In addition, students appreciate specific comments on the strengths and weaknesses of their work and a constructive challenge concerning what could yet be improved. Although these expectations could reasonably be expected to apply to all students, including those enrolled in campus-based programs, they are made more poignant by the limited face-to-face contact experienced by students at a distance. We have found that students cherish receiving prompt feedback in distance education courses because it enables them to make the necessary adjustments to achieve the expected learning outcomes. This continuing contact between the instructor and the students also contributes toward high rates of course completion.

In this section, we present some examples of strategies for providing students with feedback to help promote learning and improve performance. Before doing so, however, we must emphasize that the course syllabus should indicate clearly the time the instructor needs to review students' work and make individualized comments on assignments before the students can expect to have their work returned. Although the turnaround time is affected by class size, instructor's workload, and the number of assignments and exams, students appreciate instructors' adhering to the stated response time. This helps them plan how they will use the feedback in making the necessary changes and in proceeding with the next unit of the course.

Two additional points regarding assignment submission for feedback are worth noting: (a) The syllabus should include a reminder suggesting that students keep file copies of all material they submit until after the end of the term, and (b) any assignment sent either electronically or by postal service should be acknowledged as soon as it is received. Instructors do not have to wait until they have had a chance to evaluate a submission—a simple "I got your assignment today" message suffices. This practice both lets students rest easy knowing the instructor has received their work and provides a personal touch for a distance education course in lieu of face-to-face contact.

1. *React to students' first draft of the paper and give suggestions for making revisions.* Detailed feedback from instructors and peers helps students learn to revise and rewrite their drafts. They discover in this process that feedback is central to learning and improving performance. Providing feedback takes time, however. Instructors may save time by encouraging peer feedback, self-evaluations, and shorter papers. One strategy is to create dyads or subgroups of three or four students and have each pair or group read and comment on each other's papers using the criteria that have been included with the assignment. Students then revise their papers—even drafts—before submitting them for final grading. This approach is not at all unreasonable, given the availability of word processors and electronic mail. Although focused comments facilitate learning, their effect is twice as great if the students have a chance to revise their papers incorporating the suggestions that instructors provide (Hillocks, 1982). Following the strategy developed by Barbara Cambridge (1996), instructors may ask the students to attach three questions regarding specific items about which they seek comment or suggestions. This approach encourages students to develop the ability to evaluate their own writing and gives instructors some guidance on where to focus their comments. Another practice is to provide students with the criteria that will be used in evaluating their work. These criteria may then be used as benchmarks or targets in reviewing student papers and providing them with detailed feedback. Keeping a systematic record of these comments allows the instructor and students to monitor their development throughout the course. Some instructors assign course grades based on students' entire portfolios, rather than grading each paper separately.

2. *Encourage students to develop portfolios documenting the progress they have made in the course or the program as a whole.* Portfolios provide

students with an excellent means of documenting what has been accomplished through time. They might include early as well as later examples of student papers or other assignments to demonstrate the progress they made. In the preceding section, we noted the benefits of outlining the evaluation criteria and using them to provide students with individualized feedback on their work. Keeping a systematic record of these as a part of the course or program portfolio allows the students to monitor their progress during the course. Instructors may also ask the students to write a commentary assessing change and growth that they have experienced during the term and outlining focus areas they plan to address in the course(s) they will take in the following term. In the master of education program offered via distance education at The College of St. Scholastica, we invite students to turn in their annotated reports, papers, and assignments in a folder first as a rough draft for ungraded feedback on the portfolio that will eventually be graded. We agree with Angelo and Cross (1993) that unless the portfolio is clearly linked to other graded assignments, and is itself graded, some students will refuse to expend the time and effort it requires. In addition, we have found that all students, especially those enrolled in distance courses, appreciate receiving specific instructions on items such as papers to keep in the portfolio, questions to address in preparing the annotations, themes to emphasize in writing the synthesis, and the criteria to use in reporting their progress. To be sure, portfolios take significant student time to prepare and instructor time to assess, but they contribute substantially to increasing students' self-awareness, helping them monitor their progress, and enhancing their awareness of how they learn and how they think. These are, indeed, important skills that help students become active participants in their own learning.

3. *Create simulations and quizzes with inherent feedback.* Distance learners commonly express a lack of awareness of how well they are performing in the course, what concepts and principles they are learning, what areas they are having difficulty in mastering, and what knowledge and skills they are developing. In addition to a need for opportunities for self-assessment and prompt feedback, these students also express a need for learning activities that give them an opportunity to apply the abstract concepts and principles covered in the course. To address these needs, instructors should consider using instructional materials that include learning activities such as study questions, case

studies with questions, quizzes, exercises, and review tests. In other words, the criteria for selection of instructional materials for a distance education course are significantly different from those in choosing the materials for on-campus courses.

An online undergraduate course on aging and diversity that one of us offers includes a number of case studies with follow-up questions. Students post their responses to the discussion questions on the course Web site, review what their classmates have to say, and share their reactions with each other. In addition to using case studies, the course also includes self-tests/practice tests at the end of each unit. Students take these quizzes, check their answers with the help of the key they are provided, and restudy the areas in which they had more mistakes. Finally, the course also includes assignments in which the students pursue activities such as (a) interviewing an older adult and writing a report based on what they learned in the interview; (b) examining popular magazines and assessing how older adults from different ethnic groups are portrayed; and (c) conducting systematic observations of older adults in a shopping mall and writing a brief report summarizing what they have learned.

A number of commercial firms have created simulation software in a variety of content areas having the potential to provide valuable learning experiences to students who do not have access to a laboratory or expensive equipment. Before instructors decide to use a given simulation, we highly recommend that they experience the simulation. This allows them to assess the extent to which it matches the student learning outcomes they had envisioned, prepare their own instructions that students can easily follow, and evaluate the time needed to complete the simulation. It is also important to ensure that the students have access to the technology needed to use the simulation software.

4. *Use e-mail for providing detailed person-to-person feedback.* Regardless of the mode of course delivery (e.g., television, videotapes, audiotapes, and print materials), e-mail is a valuable tool for maintaining contact with the students and affording the instructor a ready means of providing individualized feedback, advice concerning difficulties that students may be experiencing, and suggestions for facilitating the learning process. Although communicating with the students via e-mail allows instructors to respond to their questions, address their individual learning needs, and respond to the concerns that may arise, it

does take considerable time. For this reason, it is wise to create some guidelines in this regard and include them in the course syllabus. For example, instructors may decide to (a) provide individualized feedback to each student on his or her assignments; (b) create an e-mail message for the class as a whole with the goal of sharing observations on the exams or assignments immediately after they have been graded; and (c) allow students to contact instructors if there is a need to discuss their performance on the exam they recently took. This three-part approach is similar to the approach that many instructors take in their campus-based courses. It meets students' needs for guidance and support and, at the same time, does not create heavy demands on instructor time.

Good Practice 5: Emphasize time on task.

> Time plus energy equals learning. Learning to use one's time well is critical for students and professionals alike. Allocating realistic amounts of time means effective learning for students and effective teaching for faculty. (Chickering & Gamson, 1991, pp. 19-20)

Whether students are attending on-campus classes, enrolled in a distance education course, or participating in a program in which the entire curriculum is offered via distance learning, their achievement is affected by the time and energy that they devote to course activities. To be sure, new technologies can dramatically improve student efficiency in performing various tasks. Many students, however, need training in selecting and using appropriate technology effectively and efficiently. This is especially true for distance education students who may be located in smaller communities with limited exposure to state-of-the-art technologies. If this is the population that the course plans to serve, instructors may consider providing a technology tutorial about what equipment to buy, what software to acquire, and how to accomplish tasks required in the course.

1. *Help students learn how to use technology to access learning resources.* Learning to use one's time well is critical. Students may make better use of available time when they can access learning resources through the Internet. A study guide for distance learning courses should include information on using online library catalogs, conduct-

ing literature searches through pertinent databases, and saving the relevant information from the search. Students appreciate having this information presented in a user-friendly language and style. For example, for a course in psychology, instructors may consider including in the study guide a list of selected databases available in behavioral and social sciences. Another possibility may be to include an example of an entry from the database, such as the one shown in Table 3.1 from the Educational Resources Information Center (ERIC) database.

Presenting such an example allows instructors to (a) demonstrate what information the students will be able to obtain from a search of the databases; (b) discuss what such searches can or cannot provide; and (c) explain how students should proceed after completing the initial search using their personal computer from home. Learning how to search databases is helpful to students not only in the present but also in later courses, research projects, work life, and continuing education.

2. *Include an orientation to effective study skills.* On the first day of an on-campus class, many instructors provide their students with tips on how to do well in the course. They suggest strategies such as coming to class regularly, reading the required materials, completing the given assignments on time, reviewing the notes they take in the course, finding a study partner, and meeting the instructor right away when questions arise. Including such a discussion in the beginning motivates students to do well in the course, reminds them of effective study skills, and helps them remain focused on the task at hand. Given the independent study that distance learning courses entail, a similar discussion of effective learning strategies for distance education students should be included in the course syllabus or study guide. Describe basics such as how to study independently, how to manage time and stress, how to find a study buddy, and how to make contact with the instructor. Table 3.2 is an excerpt from a section on how to study the textbook included in the syllabus for a distance education course on aging and diversity taught by one of us.

In addition to including an overview of how to study, instructors may also suggest sources available via the Internet, libraries, or bookstores. Most of these guidebooks include coverage not only of study techniques but also of time and stress management, reading, taking notes, writing papers, taking tests, and other activities that lead to improved performance. Examples of useful books on this topic include

TABLE 3.1 Database Entry From ERIC

ERIC NO: ED429558

Title: Giving Psychology Away Through Technology-Based Instruction

Author: Mehrotra, Chandra M.

Language: English

Descriptors: Access to Education; Computer Uses in Education; *Distance Education; Educational Principles; *Educational Technology; Educational Trends; Guidelines; Higher Education; *Information Technology; *Instructional Design; Lifelong Learning

Identifiers: Learner Centered Instruction; *Technology Based Instruction

Abstract: This paper outlines key features of good distance education, drawing upon principles for good practice in undergraduate education and recorded experiences with distance learning programs in a number of content areas. The first section defines distance education and provides a historical perspective. Five interrelated phenomena that have accompanied the rapid growth of information technology to promote widespread use of distance learning are described in the second section, including the emergence of lifelong learning, learning centered instruction, providing access, rapid advances in technology and the psychology of learning, and increased interest in part-time study. The third section offers recommendations for good distance education, and the last section summarizes the following lessons learned as a result of offering both undergraduate and graduate courses via distance learning: include adequate details in the syllabus, break the course into modules; conduct periodic assessment; encourage contact between students and faculty; and promote interaction between students. One figure presents a historical perspective of the phases of distance education. (DLS)

Geographic Source: U.S. Minnesota

Clearinghouse No: IR019567

Publication Type: 142; 150

Publication Date: 1998

EDRS Price: EDRS Price MF01/PC01 Plus Postage.

Comments: Paper presented at the Annual Convention of the American Psychological Association (106th, San Francisco, CA, August 14-18, 1998).

Page: 10

Level: 1

TABLE 3.2 How to Study the Textbook

Outlined below are some specific suggestions that may be helpful to you in accomplishing the course objectives effectively and efficiently. To learn the material effectively, make full use of the many distinctive features of the textbook. Please note that each chapter includes (a) a preview with orienting questions, (b) an introduction and a summary, (c) a number of vignettes with discussion questions, (d) a range of active learning exercises that involve ethnic elders, (e) quizzes and their keys, and (f) a glossary.

1. *Orienting Questions:* We suggest that you begin each chapter by reviewing the orienting questions. They provide you with an overview of the content covered in the chapter and suggest connections to be made during reading across subdivisions of the chapter. These questions are also appropriate for essay examinations; if you can write sensible meaty paragraphs to these questions, you have grasped the main themes. In addition to these orienting questions, you may also consider taking a quick look at the summary before reading the chapter itself. This will also speed up reading and improve comprehension.

2. *Discussion Questions:* Each chapter includes a number of vignettes and other active learning experiences with discussion questions. You should make an effort to complete all the learning activities. During the course you will be submitting written responses to three activities that have been chosen by your instructor. Also, each week you will be posting responses on the electronic bulletin board to discussion questions for activities selected by the instructor.

3. *Quizzes:* After you have read a given chapter, we suggest that you take the quiz provided at the end of the narrative. In addition to indicating whether a given statement is true or false, it may also be beneficial to outline why you selected a given response. In other words, you should consider items in a quiz as invitations to think about principles, issues, and research related to aging and diversity. Writing brief answers to these items and checking them with the answer key will provide valuable feedback, will allow you to monitor the progress you are making, and will enhance your understanding of the content included in the chapter.

4. *Glossary:* Following the chapter quiz is a glossary that reviews briefly the meaning of many of the technical terms included in the chapter. These short and simple statements are less formal than a dictionary definition, but they should be easy to remember. The textbook discussion of a term is usually more complete, and to locate the discussion, you should turn to the subject index. Please note that often the discussion for new concepts is divided, appearing at two or more places. Such division of material should help in learning because it provides additional information on concepts introduced earlier.

How to Study in College (Pauk, 1997), *More Learning in Less Time* (Kahn, 1998), *Studying Smart* (Scharf-Hunt & Hait, 1990), and *The Distance Learner's Guide* (Connick, 1999). Online resources include Dartmouth College's *Learning Strategy Guides* (n.d.), UCLA's *Thinking Critically About World Wide Web Resources* (Grassian, 2000), and Purdue University's *Evaluating Internet Sites* (Sharkey, 2000).

Because few of these study skills materials were designed for students enrolled in distance learning courses or programs, students will need to adapt some of the recommendations and techniques to the delivery mode that they are using. In addition, students should be reminded that beyond reading about how to study, they need to learn the study skills by putting them into practice!

Good Practice 6: Communicate high expectations.

Expect more and you will get it. High expectations are important for everyone—for the poorly prepared, for those willing to exert themselves, and for the bright and well motivated. Expecting students to perform well becomes a self-fulfilling prophecy. (Chickering & Gamson, 1991, pp. 20-21)

Communicating high expectations on a continuing basis plays a critical role in sustaining student motivation. Although communicating such expectations is important for students in all courses, it is especially important for students enrolled in distance education courses, who do not see instructors on a regular basis and may not be aware of their standards. The course goals that instructors establish, the instructional materials that they select, the teaching methods that they use, the assignments that they design, and the feedback mechanisms that they create play a critical role in providing students an indicator of what instructors expect them to learn, how to learn it, and at what level. Clearly articulating expectations in the beginning sets the tone for the course and performs a motivational function for the students. In this section, we suggest some helpful approaches for communicating high expectations to students.

Because the goals influence all the activities in the course, they should be challenging and should be communicated clearly. This discussion should not be limited to the beginning of the course but should transpire regularly in relating topics, learning activities, assignments, and assessment methods to the established goals for the course. In one of our distance education courses, the goals are included as an integral component of each learning activity. This approach allows the students to understand why they need to complete a certain assignment, what outcomes it will help them to achieve, and how they will recognize achieving the goals. Using this approach also implies the value of clearly communicating the criteria to be used for evaluating student work in each of the learning activities.

Another strategy for communicating instructor expectations to distance education students requires sharing with them samples of excellent, average, mediocre, and poor performance. These examples—drawn from the work submitted by former students (with personal identifiers deleted)—make expectations concrete, help students distinguish between different levels of performance, allow them to link assignments with the goals, and stimulate them to meet instructor expectations. It also helps to include a description of the original assignment and a commentary on why the job was rated excellent, average, and so on.

Students should be encouraged to show instructors electronically a rough draft of their papers, assignments, or project reports for comments and suggestions. Providing detailed comments on the draft itself about suggested changes allows instructors to assess the extent to which the student incorporated comments into the final version of the assignment. Experience indicates that providing detailed comments on an individualized basis is highly effective in communicating expectations, in monitoring students' progress, and in assessing students' use of feedback at various stages of the assignment.

Instructors should engage students in self-reflection and self-evaluation. All learning, especially in distance courses, is to some extent self-learning and must be self-guided and self-motivated. The more students know about themselves as learners, the better they will be at guiding their own learning. Angelo and Cross (1993) have developed a number of techniques that may be adapted to promote the development of sophisticated self-assessment skills in students. One of these techniques, the *diagnostic learning log,* may be particularly useful in distance education courses. This technique asks the students to keep a record of the process they used for each topic or assignment. For each topic, they prepare one list of the main points they understood and a second list of points that were unclear. For assignments, they record problems encountered or errors made, as well as excellent and successful responses. On a regular basis, they reflect, analyze, and summarize the information they have collected on their own learning. This helps them diagnose their strengths and weaknesses as learners and stimulates them to generate possible remedies for problems. As Angelo and Cross report, this technique encourages students to become more self-reflective, active, and independent learners. In addition, it provides the instructors with valuable data on students' metacognitive skills—their skills at observing, evaluating, and criticizing their own learning. Furthermore, monitoring of student logs will help instructors keep track of what the students do and do not understand. This information then can be used to make modifications and improvements in the instructional materials in subsequent terms in which the course is taught.

Good Practice 7: Respect diverse talents and ways of learning.

Many roads lead to learning. Different students bring different talents and styles to college. Brilliant students in a seminar might be all thumbs in a lab or studio; students rich in hands-on experience may not do so well with theory. Students need opportunities to show their talents and learning in ways that work for them. Then they can be pushed to learn in new ways that do not come so easily. (Chickering & Gamson, 1991, pp. 21-22)

Given the variability in student needs, life experiences, levels of knowledge, and approaches to learning, instructors may find it beneficial to begin collecting information regarding their students' background and preferences. Although it may not be possible to accommodate all the learning styles and preferences in teaching, instructors will do better jobs than if they know nothing about the students they will be teaching. Conducting such a survey by available technology (e-mail, mail questionnaire, etc.) also communicates personal interest in students and conveys that instructors will do their best in using the information they provide about themselves. Furthermore, completing such a survey provides the students an opportunity for self-reflection and self-assessment.

Having an awareness of students' current strengths, knowledge, and learning preferences will be helpful in selecting the learning resources, the modes of delivery, design of assignments, and assessment procedures for the course. In addition to the needs and preferences of the learners, course content, its outcomes, and the constraints faced by the instructor also affect the selection of the instructional resources and delivery system. Taking all these factors into account will most likely result in a mix of teaching tools and technology, each serving a specific purpose. For example, a distance education course may use (a) well-organized print materials that promote active learning, (b) the Internet as an information resource, (c) electronic interaction among the students and between the students and the instructor, (d) group projects, and (e) field experiences. Although this is not a comprehensive list of all possible instructional tools and technologies, it is given here to illustrate that effective teaching uses a variety of methods to help students achieve the course outcomes.

In light of the continuing increase in cultural and ethnic diversity in distance learning courses, it is important to ensure that course content (particularly in humanities and behavioral and social sciences) is inclusive of multicultural norms and intellectual interests and is sensitive to the needs of students from different ethnic groups. Increased cultural diversity in the student population provides a further impetus for making study skills and language/writing supports integral elements of the course design. Indeed, many distance education courses—whatever the delivery method—include instructional units on study skills, library research, and writing papers and project reports.

Instructors must respond flexibly to the diverse backgrounds that students bring to their study. Although rich arrays of learning techniques and information technologies have become available to support flexible learning, instructors facilitate learning by advising students on resources and modes of study that are consistent with their needs, backgrounds, learning styles, and preferences. Thus, the instructors should not only be knowledgeable about available resources, technologies, and learning strategies but also be open to accepting different ways of achieving the expected outcomes. In other words, increased diversity makes it imperative to use flexible, student-centered approaches to learning.

Summary Tips

- Provide students with an e-mail address for the instructor; encourage them to use this method for routine contact.

- Provide students with a toll-free telephone number for urgent contact.

- Moderate online discussions, summarizing main points, and indicate when it is appropriate to close a discussion and move on to another topic.

- Provide students with information needed to contact each other, consistent with privacy laws and individual choice.

- Encourage off-site work in teams to promote group learning.

- Create assignments in which students act as peer reviewers, providing feedback to each other.

- Design assignments that cause students to learn by doing.

- Provide opportunities for students to demonstrate application of skills they have learned through videotape, interactive television, live presentations, and so on.

- Acknowledge receiving assignments.

- Indicate when graded assignments are to be returned, and adhere to the schedule.

- Provide feedback on assignments—offer encouraging comments as well as corrections.

- Justify the assignment grade in relation to the comments and corrections.

- Return an assignment before another that builds on it is due to be submitted by students.

- Provide students with self-tests and other diagnostic tools for them to assess their own progress.

- Improve retention by contacting students who appear to be falling behind in meeting class obligations.

- Provide tips on effective study techniques for the course.

- Provide a tutorial on technology skills.

- Plainly state performance expectations, and reinforce those throughout the course.

- Give specific examples that translate expectations into grading practices.

- Determine student learning styles and adjust teaching method accordingly.

Www ▶ At our Sage Web site, www.sagepub.com/mehrotra

Our companion Web site provides additional examples of strategies that have been used to promote active learning in distance education courses. There are also links to online newsletters, journals, reports, and other publications illustrating creative approaches for building a community of learners and fostering student learning in distance courses.

References

Angelo, T. A., & Cross, K. P. (1993). *Classroom assessment techniques: A handbook for college teachers* (2nd ed.). San Francisco: Jossey-Bass.

Cambridge, B. (1996, December). Looking ahead. *AAHE Bulletin, 49*(4), 10-11.

Chickering, A. W., & Gamson, Z. F. (1991). Seven principles for good practice in undergraduate education. In A. W. Chickering & Z. F. Gamson, *Applying the seven principles for good practice in undergraduate education* (pp. 63-69). San Francisco: Jossey-Bass.

Connick, G. P. (Ed.). (1999). *The distance learner's guide.* Upper Saddle River, NJ: Prentice Hall.

Grassian, E. (2000). *Thinking critically about World Wide Web resources.* Los Angeles: UCLA College Library. Retrieved April 2, 2001, from the World Wide Web: www.library.ucla.edu/libraries/college/help/critical/index.htm

Hillocks, G. (1982). The interaction of instruction, teacher comment, and revision in teaching the composing process. *Research in Teaching of English, 16,* 261-278.

Kahn, N. B. (1998). *More learning in less time: A guide for students, professionals, career changers, and lifelong learners* (5th ed.). Gwynedd Valley, PA: Ways-to Books.

Learning strategy guides. (n.d.). Hanover, NH: Darmouth College. Retrieved April 2, 2001, from the World Wide Web: www.dartmouth.edu/~acskills/right_les_lsg.html

Pauk, W. (1997). *How to study in college.* Boston: Houghton Mifflin.

Scharf-Hunt, D., & Hait, P. (1990). *Studying smart: Time management for college students.* New York: HarperPerennial.

Sharkey, J. (2000). *Evaluating Internet sites.* West Lafayette, IN: Purdue University Libraries. Retrieved April 2, 2001, from the World Wide Web: www.lib.purdue.edu/InternetEval/textintro/tresources.html

4

The Syllabus for Distance Learning Courses

In this chapter, we confront several questions: What is a syllabus? Should the syllabus for a distance education course differ from one for a comparable on-campus class? If so, how? What do the seven principles for good practices in education (see Chapter 3) suggest about the construction of a syllabus? How and when should the syllabus be transmitted to the student?

Before beginning, we need to define several terms as they are used in the text. The *study guide* or *course manual* is a packet (often printed and bound) containing all the noncommercial materials that the instructor has assembled for the course. Typically, the guide contains supplementary items such as lecture notes, handouts, photocopied material (secure copyright permission!), reference lists, samples of old exams or assignments, and so on. Of course, these materials can be made available online.

The *syllabus* is the description of the nuts and bolts of the course. The *course outline* or *schedule* is the chronological listing of course activities (readings, lectures, assignments, and exams) intended to guide students to achieving mastery of course objectives. Both the syllabus and course outline are often included in the study guide.

What Is a Syllabus?

If you ask 10 faculty members to define the word *syllabus,* you are most likely to get 10 answers. Educators are not unlike the judge who wrote, "The court may not be able to define obscenity, but it knows it when it sees it." We may readily recognize a colleague's document as a syllabus but heartily disagree about what should be included in it. Perhaps this is as it should be: Just as no one size of shoe can possibly fit everyone's foot, no one style of syllabus can be appropriate for every type of class. For this reason, our approach will be suggestive, rather than prescriptive. We will describe the many elements that *could be* included in a syllabus and invite readers to decide which are the most appropriate to include or emphasize for the purposes of a particular course.

A syllabus answers the who, what, where, when, why, and how questions about a course, such as the following:

- Who should take this course? Who is teaching it? Who does a student contact for help with technology problems associated with taking the course at a distance?

- What institution is providing the course? What is this class about? What will students know and be able to do as a result of following the plan of studies for this course? What are the prerequisite or corequisite classes and experiences needed? What are the required and recommended reading materials and supplies? What is the mode of delivery of the course? What topics are covered in this class? What are the program and course policies?

- How are students evaluated? How are course grades determined? What are the grading standards?

- When are assignments due, and how are they to be submitted? What supplemental, noncredit learning activities are available to students who wish to pursue the subject further?

- Why should a student take this class? Why might it be better to take this class via distance learning rather than on-campus (or vice versa)?

- How can the instructor be contacted? How does the student at a distance access library and other support services?

More Than a List

One common view of a course syllabus regards it merely as a list of "things to remember" and "things to do." From this perspective, the document can be short, quickly written, and amended by the instructor as the course proceeds. Although this approach may work for a traditional on-campus course, it invites immediate frustration and time inefficiency in the context of a distance education course. Either students will have to be contacted with clarifications and explanations, or the instructor needs to be prepared for an avalanche of phone calls and e-mails asking for explanations.

Quite plainly, the syllabus for a distance learning course needs to be more detailed than for the corresponding on-campus course because there are more issues that must be addressed. To do otherwise is to doom students and the faculty to unnecessary frustration and wasted time. It may also result in loss of tuition revenue. (We are not implying that shoddy syllabi for on-campus courses are acceptable—but rather that distance education creates new demands that must be addressed in a syllabus.)

We suggest that the instructor and students in a distance education course view the syllabus as the organizing principle or planning document for the entire course. It can be constructed to connect the readings, assignments, course objectives, and resource materials in a coherent order that flows from the beginning to the end of the class. It need not contain information about every conceivable matter pertinent to the course, but it can point the students to the right place to obtain the information. A syllabus also provides a document that the student can submit to another institution for evaluation of transfer credit for the course.

In the remaining part of this chapter, we will demonstrate the construction of a syllabus for a hypothetical distance learning course, guided by the seven principles for good practices in education described in Chapter 3.

Outline for a Syllabus: Putting It Together

As we mentioned before, our intent here is to describe an idealized document for a course, not to pontificate. Individual instructors are the best judges of what must be included for their courses. But we repeat: It is imperative to carefully think out the whole course in advance and clearly communicate plans to students—the sooner the better. To do otherwise is to court frustration and dissatisfaction for both students and instructor.

Conversely, there is danger in making a syllabus so extensive that students fail to read it. Some of the items in the outline below might well be addressed in another document or source, for example, issues relating to the types of technology requirements for the class. We recommend, however, that the syllabus at least call attention to such items and direct the students to the other source. Thus, the syllabus can provide a lot of direction to the students without being overly long. Following is the outline of a possible syllabus.

    I.   *Identifiers.* These "headline" items constitute a miniature catalog or bulletin description of the course. Including this information provides the students with a succinct reminder of the big picture.

        A. Name of college or university sponsoring course

        B. Course number, name, and credit

        C. Term or dates this course is being offered

        D. Course description: A short paragraph should indicate what topics the course covers, whom the course is intended to serve (general audience or specific field or profession), what the course intends to provide the student as major outcomes, any prerequisites or corequisites, and its place in the sequence of a larger program, if appropriate. The description may well be the same as the copy in the

> university bulletin or catalog, but placing the thumbnail paragraph here provides a convenient reminder to the students and any reviewer who later may need to evaluate the course for transfer credit.

II. *Instructor information.* Because students may never meet face-to-face with the instructor, it is important that they do know when and how to contact the teacher. By providing some welcoming comments to students, the instructor may also make the distance education experience less impersonal and sterile.

  A. Name and position (a short description of the instructor's earned degrees and experience in the field bearing on this course may be appropriate): If the course is being team taught, the syllabus should clearly indicate if both instructors may be contacted about any aspect of the course or delineate which person is responsible for what portions of the class.

  B. Contact information: mailing address, phone number, voice mail, fax number, and e-mail address. It is a good idea to indicate both the preferred method of contact for routine business and when instructors are most likely to be in the office for immediate contact by phone. Do instructors encourage, allow, or discourage students contacting them on weekends or at home?

  C. Office hours: Will specific times during the week be dedicated for answering student questions individually or in a group? If so, when? How? Do instructors plan to reply immediately to e-mail messages at certain times? Will the course have an Internet-based chat room or message board? Will instructors make available a list of the questions that students have asked (and answers)?

III. *Technology tools.* Students need a complete description of the specific equipment required to access the course materials. If this information applies to a program as a whole, it may be better to provide the specifications in a separate document that is referred to by the syllabus.

A. How is the course instruction being delivered? What supporting equipment does a student need to access it: radio, TV-VCR, satellite link, fax, or cassette or audio reel player?

B. Do students require computers? If so, are there specific hardware requirements for input devices (parallel, serial, Universal Serial Bus [USB], FireWire, Small Computer System Interface [SCSI]); memory; operating system (DOS, Windows, Mac OS, Unix); and data retrieval (CD-ROM, DVD, high-capacity disk reader such as Zip or Jaz)? Does the student need an Internet connection? If so, what is the minimum speed? Is a specific Web browser, file transfer program, or word processor required? Are these provided to students, or are students expected to acquire these on their own? Is there campus support for long-distance learners' technology-related questions? If so, who? And how are they contacted? Are any specific software packages required for the course? If so, what are the memory requirements?

C. Do students enrolled in distance learning courses have campus computer network privileges for e-mail and other software? If so, how do they go about setting up an account and accessing it? Is technical support service available off-campus, and if so, how?

IV. *Course materials.* Students need to know before the course starts exactly what supplies they minimally need to complete the course successfully and when in the course they will be used. It is also important to distinguish between materials supplied or lent out as part of the tuition and those that require further financial expenditure by students.

A. What books, videos, printed materials, specialized supplies, and so on are required (i.e., essential to meet the minimum demands of the course)? Where and how are students to obtain these? For example, are they available for order as a complete package under the name of the course through the university bookstore or the department offering the course? For what cost? Are taxes and shipping charges included? Can these be ordered online or by e-mail? Are any of the materials being sent on loan, to be returned at the end of the course, or will the bookstore buy back any used materials for resale? Alternatively, these materials can be placed on a course Web site or electronic library—but copyright permissions should be secured well in advance of when the materials are used in the course.

B. If students are not ordering a prepackaged set of materials, it is imperative that the syllabus provide complete information for ordering: name of item, author, edition, publication date, publisher, ISBN number, Library of Congress number, vendor, and price. It is also a good idea to indicate the order in which the materials are needed in case students are not able to secure all the supplies at once. (Check that all materials are indeed on hand at the campus bookstore or outside vendor before the course starts. If students are responsible for securing materials on their own, make plans for how to address the needs of those who say they "can't get the stuff.")

C. Are there supplemental recommended materials that students may find useful? If so, for what? Indicate those that the students may find most useful. Again, provide the necessary ordering information.

V. *Help with the coursework.* Students routinely approach the instructor with "how do I . . ." questions before or after class on campus. To reduce students' frustration with accomplishing the basic educational goals of the course and to minimize the time spent in contacting students about housekeeping chores, it is important to inform students at the beginning of the course of all the resources they could reasonably be expected to need in completing their work.

A. Tips on how to study or approach this class: Instructors are more than dispensers of information and graders of assignments. An instructor not only shows students *what* to study in a given area but provides guidance about *how* the material can be most appropriately approached. (See Table 3.2 in Chapter 3 for a specific example.) Assuredly, not all students have the same learning style. Even so, the teacher of a distance education course can greatly facilitate the progress of the students by passing on suggestions about how to do the work. Not all the students will be experienced at distance learning. Some things that seem obvious to the teacher are not obvious to the students looking at the course for the first and only time. Perhaps the instructor has gained some insights from previous experience with other students taking the class at a distance that can be passed along. For example,

- About how many hours a day or week should students expect to spend on the coursework?

- What are the most important activities in the course?

- How can students organize the time spent on the course most effectively?

- How should students organize their questions before contacting the instructor?

- If there is no lecture to attend, why take notes? On what? And how?

- What is the recommended way to approach the readings?

- How should students prepare for exams in this course?

B. Library resources: Students may need to know how to access reference materials at a distance. Describe how journal articles, reserve materials, and general circulation works can be secured from the university library or through interlibrary loan.

C. Search services and databases: Are there Internet-based database tools that students should be aware of and know how to access? Do students understand the difference between scholarly database search engines and those such as Yahoo! and Excite that may point to nonrefereed material of questionable value?

D. Tutorial and counseling assistance: Is help available on campus in person or at a distance with writing, personal development, or other matters that affect course performance but that are not provided by the instructor directly? Is supplemental learning material on reserve in the library or online? What are the hours and phone number of the bookstore? Is there a contact person for distance education courses in the bookstore? If financial aid is available to distance learners, to whom should student inquiries be directed? (See also Chapter 7.)

E. Frequently asked questions: Perhaps some procedural or content-related questions seem to recur each time the course is taught on campus or at a distance. These could be treated in a FAQ section, or better, students could be directed by the syllabus to a Web site handling these questions and their answers.

VI. *Policies and legal issues.* When both the instructor and students know the "rules of the game" before play starts, both parties are better served.

A. College or university policies that govern all courses offered by the institution need not be reiterated in detail in the syllabus. References to the appropriate pages in the official bulletin or catalog are sufficient, provided students have access to them.

B. Policies particular to this course must be explicated in an unambiguous manner to avoid confusion or possible confrontation with students. This suggestion provides guidance for the students, communicates instructor expectations, reduces unnecessary argumentation, and offers the instructor some protection from being considered capricious. A statement (a disclaimer) could be included saying that the instructor can make adjustments in the plan of the course if need arises. For example,

- When is an assignment late? If it is due on a particular date, does it become late at the close of the business day, after the instructor goes home, after the last mail delivery, or at midnight?

- What is the penalty for work being submitted late? Under what extenuating circumstances would the instructor waive a penalty (if at all)?

- What is the instructor's interpretation of the university academic honesty policy? Yes, plagiarism and other misrepresentation of authorship are dishonest, but the limits on receiving "help" on assignments from an outside source should be specified. When students are permitted to work together, must the collaborators be named and the extent of contributed effort be delimited? Some of these issues certainly can be covered in detail in the direct context of a specific assignment.

- Is it permissible for students to consult the work of other students who have previously completed the course? For example, are old exams or assignments legitimate study aids?

C. Special accommodations: The Americans With Disabilities Act of 1990 requires that universities and colleges receiving federal funds (pretty much all) make reasonable accommodations to those students seeking access to educational services. Long-distance education programs must comply with these regulations as well. Students need to be told whom to contact about arranging necessary accommodation for special needs and when. In some institutions, the contact may be the instructor; in others, the authority may be a committee or designated administrative officer who decides if the request is "reasonable" and suggests what accommodations the instructor is required to make for the student (see Chapter 7).

VII. *Evaluation and grading.* When people know that they will be rewarded or punished for certain behaviors, they quite reasonably adjust their actions to maximize their rewards or minimize punishment. Not surprisingly, students want to know how to allocate their efforts in completing assignments. Fairness to students dictates that they be told the bottom line in a course. (The instructor's own self-interest is served as well: Why set oneself up to possible charges of arbitrary grading?) The weight allocated to each assignment or activity should reflect the relative importance attached to the outcome it is designed to assess. Students need to know the following:

A. How is the final course grade determined?

B. When are assignments due, when are they returned, and how much does each contribute toward the final grade computation?

C. If there are exams, are they taken on-campus, off-campus with a proctor, off-campus under the honor system, or at a designated off-campus site? Who is responsible for making arrangements with off-campus sites and proctors? Are any special security protocols to be followed?

D. What is the instructor's definition of A, B, C, D, and F work? What are some examples of work considered exemplary, average, and unsatisfactory? If work is of inferior quality, do students have opportunities for recouping lost points, or are the evaluations limited to the announced assignments? Are grades assigned on an absolute scale (independent of other students' performance) or determined in relation to the other students in the present or past classes of the same course? Can grading standards be expressed as a rubric or other tool that defines criteria for grading and evaluation?

E. What penalties (if any) are assigned for work submitted late? Will the instructor simply refuse to accept the assignment, assess a fixed debit to the grade each day, or lower the grade according to a sliding scale proportional to the number of days late and the value of the assignment?

F. If circumstances beyond the control of the student prevent completion of coursework before the end of the term, what are the policies about "incomplete" grades and extensions?

G. What should students do if they do not receive a satisfactory answer about the way in which their work has been evaluated? Are there grievance or appeal procedures to be observed?

VIII. *Course content, learning objectives, and assignment schedule.* Finally, we get to the heart and soul of the course. The syllabus at this point is much like a personal map drawn up in detail by a travel club to help a driver navigate a set of unfamiliar roads between two distant cities. If followed conscientiously, the driver *should* be able to arrive at the intended destination with much less aggravation than if left to his or her devices. After all, the guides are familiar with the road conditions, any detours, interesting places along the way, and decent accommodations. The syllabus is *the* road map for students navigating the journey through the course.

A. The instructor-guide must carefully organize the schedule of readings, assignments, and activities before the course begins to provide students a reasonable opportunity to achieve the intended course outcomes—if, like the traveler, they stay alert and follow the trip plan prepared for them. Before launching a course for tuition-paying students, the instructor may want to give it a dry run with some willing guinea pigs or a review by an experienced distance educator to detect any major pitfalls that might have been overlooked.

B. Outlines for courses delivered by ITV linking a remote audience with an on-campus class are not radically different from the on-campus version. Students need to know what topic is being covered on a particular day and what preparation they should make for the class. If laboratories or sessions physically require students to be on-campus, the syllabus should state the times and places for the meetings. If possible, several labs or on-campus activities can be scheduled on the same day to use students' time on campus most efficiently. (Allowance for travel to and from the campus should be considered when setting starting and ending times.)

C. When a course is delivered asynchronously, students do not gather as a community to see or hear the instructor, but this does not rule out having shared experiences as part of the course. As we pointed out in Chapter 3 on good practices, students benefit from opportunities to interact with each other and the instructor. To this end, the instructor may choose to set up a discussion board or chat room to facilitate class participation. In this case, the course schedule should denote the dates, times, subjects, and preparation required for these group interactions. Students should understand whether everyone needs to gather online at the same time or merely "pop in" during a specified period. The instructor should also indicate how participation in these virtual meetings contributes to a student's grade: required or not? If required, how are student contributions assessed—on the quantity and/or quality of the comments? What options do students have if they are unable to participate in the group exercise?

D. When a course has little or no interaction among the participants, students have more flexibility about the time of day that each devotes to class activities, but most will benefit from having the instructor suggest the approximate or proportional time to spend on individual segments of the course. This is especially important if students are permitted to submit assignments at the conclusion of the course, rather than on a schedule throughout the course.

E. Students benefit from having a chronological big-picture view of the course before a detailed schedule is presented. For example, if five major concepts are developed in the course, these can be used as unit or section titles, with brief explanations of how the units are interrelated. If the units must be attempted in a particular sequence, rather than independently of each other, instructors should make this clear, present the schedule in this order, and explain the logic of the progression. Similarly, within a unit or section, instructors should clearly delineate any necessary order in which the work must be approached, or indicate if this is simply a suggested sequence.

F. Increasingly, consumer students, taxpayers, and accrediting agencies alike want to know what a course "is good
for": What knowledge, attitudes, and skills are the outcomes achieved by students successfully completing this
course? Providing this information is both good practice
and politically savvy. But where? Some faculty append a
list of learning objectives to their syllabi or provide them as
a separate document. We believe that it is important to
associate the learning objectives intimately with the particular activities in a section or unit of the course. The distance educator will not have the luxury of standing in front
of the students each day to call attention to a separate list of
objectives, whether it is included later in the syllabus or is a
separate document entirely. In our experience, the connection between what the students are being asked to do and
the intended result is most obvious to the learners when
the syllabus is organized to show the following for each
section or unit:

- Learning objectives

- Readings and activities

- Assignments and their specifications, due dates, contribution to the course grade, and expected date for return
  once assessed

Other Issues

When and how should the students receive the syllabus? Traditionally,
syllabi are distributed the first day of class on campus, with instructors
often spending that meeting reviewing the course outline and procedures and answering questions about the mechanics of the course. Unless students come to the campus for an orientation or the instructor is
teaching live by interactive technology, this is not a viable option. We
suggest that students receive either a paper copy of the syllabus by
mail, a copy sent by e-mail, or instructions for obtaining online access
to a syllabus *as soon as they have been registered for the course.* This requires close collaboration between the registrar and the sponsoring de-

partment or instructor but is well worth the effort. First, students may discover that the course is not appropriate to their needs and have time to drop it before the term starts. This enhances retention and reduces effort spent on students who probably would not be able (or willing) to complete the course. Second, early distribution of the syllabus also provides students ample opportunity to peruse the course plan and clear up any questions before the course gets in full swing. Third, making the syllabus available as early as practical is both good teaching and business practice: It reciprocates the interest that the students have shown in the institution.

Students, like the rest of us, often lose things. We suggest that instructors provide an online version of the current syllabus that students can download or make provision for sending replacements by fax or mail on short notice.

Syllabi posted on Web sites can be static duplicates of the paper version or can be made interactive. To make the syllabus viewable directly on a Web page, the document has to be encoded in HTML format before loading onto the server. Printing copies off a Web page can be tedious for students with slow modem connections. Even if a viewable copy is posted, a much faster way to provide a hard copy of the syllabus is to set up a compressed file in a portable document format (PDF) such as created by Adobe Acrobat. File transfer is much faster, and the same formatting as the original is retained. If the instructor and students are using the same word processing program, a compressed text file can also be provided on the Web site for downloading, but this method more likely will result in technical difficulties for students using different operating systems.

For courses that are delivered primarily through Web browsers, the syllabus can be the home page for the class, linking students directly to all materials specifically associated with a particular section of the course. Alternatively, the course home page may have hyperlinks to the syllabus, calendar, and all other sites relevant to the course.

Summary Tips

- Provide the syllabus as soon as students are registered.
- Make the syllabus the organizing document for the entire course.

- Clearly state all policies and assignments in the syllabus, or have the syllabus refer students to other sources of explicit information.

- Do not anticipate making significant changes in the syllabus once the course starts.

- Plan to deliver the syllabus in more than one format.

- If the course is delivered through a Web browser, the syllabus can be designed as the home page for the course. If not, be sure to provide a prominent link to the syllabus from the course home page.

WWw ▸   At our Sage Web site, www.sagepub.com/mehrotra

On our companion Web site are examples of course syllabi for actual distance education courses, suggestions for alternate presentations of syllabi, and templates that you can copy to speed up your own work.

5

Delivery Methods
for Distance Education

Although distance learning sometimes may seem to be a new development in education, it is not: Recall the often maligned correspondence courses of days past. What makes distance learning seem new is the development and wide availability of new technologies for connecting learner and instructor; the rapid pace at which these technologies have been adopted by educational, governmental, and commercial organizations; and widespread publicity. Used expertly, these new technologies facilitate the creation of educational experiences that are equivalent or superior to the analogous on-campus course, reach wider audiences, and better meet the needs of modern society. Used poorly, these new technologies simply result in high-technology correspondence courses.

This chapter examines the methods available for delivery of distance education, with an emphasis on the strengths and weaknesses,

69

advantages and disadvantages, of each. Our treatment is meant to be purely descriptive, rather than a how-to manual. The next chapter examines issues related to selecting and implementing appropriate delivery methods in distance education.

Traditional classroom-based instruction requires the instructor and student to meet in a particular place at a designated time. As its name implies, distance education accommodates geographic or physical separation between teacher and learner. But distance education also affords the instructor and student choices about *when* the learning exchange occurs. So before examining specific methods of instructional delivery, we direct our attention first to the temporal relationship between teacher and student.

Synchronous or Asynchronous?

When Joe Student is sitting in the classroom at the same time that Professor Drudge is presenting his lecture, the mode of instructional delivery is *synchronous*—the student "receives instruction" *at the same time* that the teacher is "delivering instruction"—even if Joe Student is reading a copy of the new issue of *Sports Illustrated* while Professor Drudge listlessly reads from yellowed notes as his sole teaching effort. (Learning is no more the same as receiving instruction than teaching is the same as delivering instruction.)

If later that evening, Jennifer Scholar listens to a tape recording of Professor Drudge's lecture (no doubt made by Joe Student), the instruction has been received *at a different time* than it was delivered—the mode of delivery is *asynchronous.* Clearly, Professor Drudge did not intend asynchronous delivery of his lecture, but a student attentively following his lecture in the auditorium has no educational advantage over Jennifer Scholar carefully listening to the tape in her dorm room. Indeed, Jennifer Scholar has the advantage of being able to go back and listen again to portions of the lecture that she did not immediately grasp on first hearing.

Some further elaboration on the preceding comments is important. Although the terms *synchronous* and *asynchronous* describe how teacher and learner are linked in time when instruction is delivered, a synchronous method should also allow two-way communication at the same time. When Joe Student attends Professor Drudge's lecture, student-teacher interaction is possible, even if it does not occur. In this text, we use the term *synchronous delivery* only for methods that incorporate simultaneous two-way communication.

Before Gutenberg's invention of movable type, printed materials were expensive and scarce; most instruction, even in the early universities, was based on oral transmission of knowledge, thus requiring learner and teacher to meet in the same physical space. Even when printed materials became more common, educational systems continued to develop along the model of teacher and student working together in the same room at the same time—synchronously—because there was no other way for the teacher to be able to provide the student immediate feedback, answer questions, or make rapid adjustments in teaching methods to meet the needs of the learner.

Today, instantaneous communication between two persons anywhere on earth is possible, widely available, and affordable. Do students and teachers still need to gather together at specified times and places to engage in education? Clearly, the answer is no. Do students and teachers still need to communicate? The evidence presented in Chapter 3 on good practices in education demonstrates that teacher-student and student-student interaction is essential for the maximum educational benefit to accrue to the student.

Education in its broadest sense is more than the accumulation of knowledge and technical skills. As social creatures, humans need to gather and interact. In large measure, education at the lower grade levels is as much about learning to get along with other people, growing into notions of acceptable public behavior, and developing a sense of self within the group as it is about learning to read, write, and compute. Even at the college and university level, cocurricular activities have come to be understood as a necessary part of the experience of earning a degree. Synchronous on-campus education, however, is no longer the best way for all persons to further their intellectual development. Changes in society, such as the rise of single-parent families, the shift from a purely industrial-based economy to one emphasizing services and information, the frequency with which people change careers, and the desire for lifelong learning, have created a new class of learners for whom seat time in the campus classroom is no longer the preferred or best way to attain their educational objectives.

Technology now affords humanity the opportunity to meet societal needs for more widespread education at potentially lower cost, for more specific and narrow audiences, and under circumstances better suited to the needs of diverse learners with varying life situations. The challenge for educators is to find the proper combination of technologies that best mimics the master-apprentice approach, which has historically worked so well. Meeting this challenge requires an understanding of what technologies are compatible with synchronous or asynchronous delivery of instruction, what the associated costs (in the widest sense, not simply economic) and benefits of each are, and how well the technology serves the educational purpose. The following sections attempt to address these points, which are then summarized in tables at the conclusion of the chapter.

Synchronous Delivery Methods

Two-way radio, telephone, interactive television, and Internet conferencing are common examples of synchronous technologies for distance education. For many years, children living on remote ranches in Australia have been schooled at home, guided by professional teachers through *two-way radio*. Relatively simple equipment is needed; the transmitter must be strong enough to cover only the distances separating student and teacher. The times and frequencies for radio communication need to be established in advance, unless the broadcast frequency is constantly monitored. Radio contact allows one teacher to assist many more students more frequently than would be possible if travel to each remote site were required.

Radio-based communication is essentially restricted to audio only. If visual aids are being used, it is necessary for both parties to view the materials simultaneously and talk through any descriptions required. The number of students that a single instructor can assist by two-way radio depends on how often contact occurs, the duration of each session, and the number of parties who can communicate at the same time and frequency without confusion. Radio communication of this type is not private—anyone tuned to the proper frequency can listen in—and it is subject to disruption by atmospheric disturbances.

Telephone links have been used for many years to keep home- or hospital-bound children up to date with their schooling in urban areas. A speaker phone is set up in the classroom and at the student's location, and the line is kept open during instructional periods. The homebound student can hear the teacher's comments to the class and follow along with work being done out loud; the child can also participate in discussions and questioning. The teacher needs to make a conscious effort to draw the isolated student into the classroom conversation. As with radio communication, both parties need to be looking at identical copies of visual aids and talk through any needed descriptions or explanations. A companion fax line can facilitate exchange of printed materials.

At the college and university level, the telephone has been used in teaching languages both for private, instructor-to-student sessions and for group instruction via conference calls. Private instruction is time-consuming for the instructor if many students are enrolled but relatively inexpensive. In contrast, class meetings held by conference call may be time efficient but require expensive telecommunications equipment and do not easily allow individual attention (Young, 2000a). Telephone service can also be used for asynchronous delivery of instruction as discussed in the next section.

Although telephonic communication is a mature technology, there are several drawbacks for its extended use in distance education. First, telephone service must be available (by line, cell, radio, or satellite connection). If regular phone service is desired at each location in addition, a line dedicated to the instructional link may be required. The number of students who can be simultaneously served by telephone is limited by the number of parties who can be connected to the instructor's location, the time required to address the specific needs of each individual, and the expense of the connections. (This also assumes that the students are all receiving the same content.) If the conversation is to be recorded for later use—for example, by those students who could not participate at the appointed time—written release and permission must be secured from the speaking participants.

Interactive television (ITV) represents current state-of-the-art technology for synchronous distance education. Both the instructor and student locations are equipped with a video-audio uplink and monitors; often, each site also has a monitor to observe the local outgoing broadcast. Signals for ITV are usually transmitted along a network of fiber-optic cables maintained by a consortium of public and private institutions within a specific geographic area. Ground to satellite to ground linking is also possible. In addition to the remote students, there may be a class audience at the instructor's location, which helps make the professor's teaching appear more relaxed and natural than if the professor were in the remote studio alone. The instructor must remember to consciously involve the remote students in the local class, however, and students in both locations need to act as if the others were in the same classroom, for instance, by not talking during question-and-answer periods between the different sites.

Several features make ITV attractive for distance education. The face-to-face exchange of both visual and auditory information provided by ITV is potentially an intellectually more stimulating process than audio-only delivery methods. Students in remote areas can have live access to needed educational opportunities that otherwise might entail frequent long trips, and institutions can expand the range of their course offerings by sharing faculty. For example, several far-flung campuses belonging to the Minnesota State College and University system in the northern part of the state offer organic chemistry lecture classes taught via ITV by one instructor; laboratory sections are held locally. A campus with low enrollment in the subject can afford students access to the course without having to hire another faculty member or require the instructor or students to travel. Similarly, Indiana University at Bloomington has been using ITV as a component in its continuing education program for in-service teachers in rural areas; participating teachers can gather at several regional sites for videoconferencing with faculty on-campus and at other remote sites (Rodes, Knapczyk, Chapman, & Chung, 2000).

ITV technology is not inexpensive. At each location, a room must be equipped with the appropriate lighting, cameras, and microphones; technical support personnel are needed to set up and maintain the equipment and provide training to the faculty; and there are annual fees for maintaining and administering the system linking the various network sites. To be cost-effective, the ITV facility should be used to the fullest extent possible.

Internet conferencing refers to any method using text, graphics, audio, and/or video transmitted by an Internet connection that allows two or more individuals to communicate in real time (i.e., synchronously). Although each of these techniques can be provided by a separate program, they are often parts of an integrated package. For example, Netscape Communicator Conference includes options for chat, a whiteboard, and audio conferencing. Microsoft NetMeeting affords options for chat, both audio and videoconferencing, a whiteboard, program sharing, and file transfers. To participate in an Internet conference, one party must initiate the "call" to the others' addresses, who must already be online or connected to the Internet.

Chat is essentially instant e-mail. Messages are sent as text and posted in a window on a Web page, and the sender is identified by name (or pseudonym). As each person in the conference sends a comment, his or her name and message appears. Everyone in the conference is a party to the e-mail postings. Some conferencing systems allow one party to send a message *sub rosa* to another during a chat. The conversation can be saved for later posting and reading (at which point communication becomes asynchronous—perhaps a form of electronic eavesdropping?).

Audio conferencing requires each participant to have a computer equipped with microphone and speakers. To use audio conferencing, the sound files being sent must be of the streaming type, that is, as soon as the files arrive at the destination, the program begins to play them. Earlier methods for transmission of audio and video files required that the entire file be transferred to the recipient before play could start.

Videoconferencing requires a digital camera (color or black-and-white), usually perched on the top of the computer's monitor. Video appears in a small window in part of the screen. The video files are compressed and streaming. Compressed sound or video files do not transmit every bit of the original sound or video shot. Depending on the compression algorithm used, sound or images are sampled at discrete intervals rather than continuously. This reduces the quantity of data that must be transmitted. For video files, only those elements that change from one scan to the next are sent out digitally, and the number of frames per second is generally smaller than the 30 to 32 frames per second required for the human eye to perceive the change as smooth, continuous motion. Hence, the video transmission is kept to a small block, and motion appears jerky. The audio and video also may not be perfectly synchronized, which may prove distracting to some users because facial expression and lip movement will not match the sound.

A *whiteboard* is a window in which graphic images are posted live during a conference; sketches displayed in the conference whiteboard area can be modified or "doodled on" by the participants, sometimes in different colors to identify the person making the marks. As with the chat transcripts, the whiteboard may be saved as a file for later viewing. This tool is particularly useful for discussions in which abstract ideas are made more clear by reference to a picture or graph, such as in math, science, psychology, and economics courses.

To illustrate, six professors from six colleges belonging to the Associated Colleges of the South have offered an advanced Latin course together. At a prearranged time, students and professors from the participating schools gather at their respective campuses to hear a live online audio broadcast of a lecture by one of the faculty members. Questions and comments are shared during the lecture time using text chat. Outside the conference class, a continuing discussion is held online, and students and faculty from each participating campus gather together for a traditional class meeting on their home campus (Young, 2000b).

Stanford Online is a program of the Stanford Center for Professional Development dedicated to delivering graduate-level classes in engineering and computer sciences to working professionals via the Internet or corporate local networks. Students can receive live lectures as streaming video (or view them later); professors or teaching assistants provide tutoring live through the Internet. The latter tutoring is truly synchronous delivery (DiPaolo, 1999).

Of the conferencing components described, the chat and whiteboard functions are the least high-tech and are least dependent on having a high-speed Internet connection. When Internet conferencing is appropriate in a distance education program, these two tools probably can suffice for most needs.

Asynchronous Delivery Methods

The tools available for asynchronous delivery of instruction are more numerous than those for synchronous delivery and range from low-tech tried-and-true methods to the latest and most advanced technologies. The presentation below roughly follows the order of increasing technological complexity.

Printed materials exchanged by mail (or other delivery service) represent one of the oldest and least expensive methods of delivering distance education. These range from simple sheets of text to commercially published books with elaborate artwork. During the past several decades, the expense of producing quality black-and-white documents (and even those with color) has fallen even as the quality of the finished product has increased. Instructors or institutions can produce highly tailored documents for their courses: the text, programmed self-study guides, visual aids, workbooks, and so on.

A drawback to using printed materials is the speed at which the materials can be revised. Textbook publishers commonly operate on a 2- to 4-year revision cycle, so recent changes in a field may not be reflected in the current edition of the text. In contrast, documents produced in-house can be updated more frequently, particularly if the source files are kept in word processor format. Thus, many instructors supplement commercial texts with manuals, worksheets, and other documents that they have authored and published in-house. Revisions by the publisher may entail reworking such instructor-authored printed materials to maintain content compatibility and optimal learning for students. Careful planning is needed to avoid accumulating stockpiles of out-of-date publications.

Students can obtain course materials, submit assignments, and receive feedback in written form through mail or delivery service. Printed materials are reasonably accessible but bulky; postage and shipping costs can be a significant expense. Also, the speed with which materials can be conveyed through the postal service limits the rate at which student and instructor can be in contact. Although overnight or next-day delivery is now available in many locations, its expense precludes use as a routine method of sending and receiving materials.

Audiotapes are especially useful for recording lectures, music, and step-by-step instructions to lead a learner through a procedure relatively hands-free, for example, a training tape for a computer program or instrument or for providing travel instructions.

Traditionally, audio recordings have been in analog format on magnetic tape reels or cassettes. Cassette players are widely accessible, often being included as part of inexpensive portable music players or boom boxes. Equipment for making the original analog recordings is available in various levels of technical sophistication, excellence, and expense. For example, a lecture can be recorded directly during a class period or out of class in a studio. A recording made during a class period is certainly easy to make and permits student questions and comments to be recorded as well. Stray ambient noise will also be recorded, however; this may be a serious distraction to the remote listener or simply be regarded as a sign of a poor-quality distance education program. The alternatives are to edit out the noise later or record the lecture minus student comments under controlled conditions. If the lecture or performance being recorded is to be used for more than one course cycle, it is probably better to make a master recording under studiolike conditions. Typical student questions or comments and instructor responses can be included either as paper copy, a companion list of frequently asked questions, or a narration by the instructor alone at the end.

Copies for distribution to students are produced by a tape duplicator, which records from the original to multiple blank tapes at the same time. If a large number of copies is needed, or tapes are rarely used in the distance education program, contracting out the duplication to a commercial recording studio may be more cost-effective and certainly less stressful than purchasing a duplicator, blank tapes and cases, and paying an operator. Allowances also need to be made for the expense and time to prepare labels, affix them to the cassettes, and insert the cassettes into protective cases.

Most boom boxes also contain built-in microphones, thus allowing students to record examples of their pronunciation skills for language classes, samples of musical performances, or speeches. Of course, in these cases, all nonverbal nuances would be absent, and the quality of the recording may be poor unless an external microphone is used.

As an alternative to cassettes, sound files can be recorded as well on CD-ROM disks as described later. Portable CD players are relatively inexpensive and popular, and the disks store much larger amounts of data than do the cassettes.

Digital recording technology is newer but becoming increasingly important. The issue has recently received much notoriety because of the successful civil suit brought by recording artists against the owners of a Web site through which anyone could download digital copies (MP3 format) of current music onto the hard drives of their computers and thence to small portable players without paying royalty fees. The situation is further complicated by the existence of competing standards for delivery of digital sound. RealNetworks offers the RealAudio format for streaming audio via the Internet (meaning the music plays as it downloads, rather than being completely downloaded before play can begin); Microsoft offers the Windows Media format; and a new, royalty-free open source format called Vorbis has been recently introduced (Borland, 1999).

Instructors who anticipate using an audio production (either selected portions or in its entirety) protected by copyright law, such as musical performances, spoken books, or broadcasts, should become familiar with relevant copyright laws. Typically, permissions must be obtained from the copyright holder, and royalty payments may be required for repeated use of a copyright-protected work.

Telephone service may be used asynchronously in several ways. Short lessons may be delivered by a recorded message; for example, samples of correct foreign language pronunciation can be recorded for students to dial up. With the appropriate telephone answering equipment, students can record spoken responses to questions after a prompt (Young, 2000a).

Facsimile (fax) machines transmit text and graphics via telephone lines, permitting students to send and receive assignments. For example, a student could receive an exam by fax at a prearranged time and be required to return the completed test within a given period. Although fax machines are not yet everyday household appliances, they are readily available at many public sites. If students submit assignments by fax, we suggest dedicating a separate phone line to the task. In addition, staff should make sure that the fax machine is stocked with sufficient paper before leaving the office for extended periods, such as weekends. Students will not appreciate having to resubmit "missing" work caused by lack of paper in the printer.

Videocassette recordings are particularly useful for distance learning. It seems as if nearly everyone owns a television set equipped with a videocassette recorder-player (VCR). For example, an on-campus class is recorded for distance viewing. The tape might be sufficiently complete to be used for individual stand-alone instruction, it might be used in conjunction with an instructor-prepared guide, or it might be viewed at a remote site by a group with a local group leader or facilitator.

Just as educators can disseminate lessons by video recordings, students can submit videos to document their skill at public speaking, foreign language pronunciation and conversation, conducting interviews, musical performance, and so forth (Carr, 2000). In this sense, the video camera and tape player become instruments for submitting assignments and making assessments of student performance. Video cameras

are not yet everyday household items, however. Instructors who anticipate having students submit video recordings should include a notice
in the course syllabus or course materials provided at the beginning of
the term, make arrangements for students to borrow or rent the cameras, and provide a level of instruction in using the cameras appropriate to the level of quality expected in the final recording.

On the production side, easy-to-use, high-quality cameras for recording to tape have become remarkably cheaper in recent years. Although adequately serviceable tapes may be neither difficult nor expensive to produce, broadcast-quality recordings require considerably
more talent, time, and money. Few students expect classroom videos to
be like Hollywood productions, but all students have the right to expect that the quality of the recording does not interfere with or detract
from the intended learning objectives. We suggest that this is the standard by which distance educators judge the videocassette recordings
they produce or use in their programs.

At the minimum, the camera should remain focused on the speaker
or visual aids. Charts, blackboard notes, and other visual aids should
be plainly visible; the video should have no "jitters"; and the speaker
should be plainly audible and extraneous noise minimized. These criteria can be met by having the camera mounted on a swiveling tripod to
follow a moving speaker; using an external microphone feed to the
camera rather than the built-in microphone; and running a test tape to
check the appropriateness of the room lighting, acoustics, and volume
settings before recording the class. This means that a camera technician
is needed also. Lecture classes are most compatible with the format just
described; questions or comments from students may not be completely audible under these circumstances, however, so it is better if the
instructor repeats the remark for the tape before responding. The tape
will be of even better quality if the classroom used for the recording is
designed to deaden ambient and external noise, has adjustable lighting, and allows amplification of questioners' voices. Any announcements or instructions that are pertinent only to the audience present for
the original recording should be either edited out of the final tape or delivered when the camera is off. Finally, if any students appear or are
heard on the videotape, their written permission may be needed before
distributing the recording.

Instructors should practice working in front of the camera to become less self-conscious about being taped. We suggest that the in-

structor view a tape of his or her teaching to become aware of and correct any mannerisms or habits that could prove distracting to students.

The highest-quality video recordings, such as those sold commercially for training tapes, are made in a studio using more than one camera, with the actors working from a script under the guidance of a director. The final tape is also usually edited.

Duplication decks for simultaneously making multiple copies of a videocassette recording are essential if videotapes are to be a major delivery component of a distance education program. Earlier comments about choosing to duplicate audiotapes in-house or with an outside contractor are equally applicable to videocassettes, as are the comments regarding labeling, mailing, and returning the tapes. In addition, there are several formats for recording video, three of the most common being NTSC (North America and Asia), PAL, and SEACAM (Europe). If the distance education program will be exported using videos, the format used in the intended service area should be determined (FJM Multimedia, 1999).

Increasingly, digital video recorders are becoming common and will supplant analog camcorders in the near future. Digital video cameras afford rapid, direct transfer of both still and moving pictures to storage on a computer hard drive. Standard VHS and 8-mm tape recorders require an analog-to-digital converter to effect the conversion, which is slower. Once the digital video has been captured to the computer hard drive, the footage can be edited and special effects added with computer software. The completed product is then ready to be exported as a VHS videocassette or a digital videodisc (DVD) or sent out through the Internet (see discussion later in this chapter). Because much of this technology has been developed and marketed with home consumers in mind, the cameras and software are designed to be user-friendly and not too expensive for an educational institution. As recent history has shown, the power and sophistication of digital video recording and hardware and software will continue to increase, even as prices show a modest decrease through time.

The preceding remarks refer to video recordings created by the educational institution. It is equally possible to incorporate commercial videos, either single programs or entire series, in distance education courses. Whether these videos are copies of programs broadcast on commercial or public television or productions obtained from companies specializing in education, appropriate licensing arrangements must be made before incorporating them into distance programs.

Radio and television broadcasts have a long history of use in education and entertainment. Indeed, advertisers have long recognized radio as the most cost-efficient way to reach the largest audience. Broadcast technology is nearly 100 years old and does not require a large infrastructure such as is needed for telephone service; an electrical plant need be available only at the broadcast station. The development of inexpensive portable transistor radios and the launching of telecommunications satellites made it possible for the government of India in the 1960s to promote family planning on a large scale. Public health education aimed at preventing the spread of HIV/AIDS has been disseminated on a wide scale in Africa.

By its nature, education transmitted by radio is broad in scope but is not well suited for providing individualized instruction or feedback to the learner. Radio is best used when little additional follow-up is needed or when it is used in conjunction with an on-site instructor, such as in a village school.

Like radio, television is excellent for reaching large populations without providing personalized instruction or feedback. The added visual dimension makes it possible to demonstrate techniques at a distance that can be grasped only by watching someone in the act as opposed to just hearing about it on the radio. Stand-alone television and radio programs are most likely to be useful distance education technologies when the learning objectives are narrow in focus and have built-in self-evaluation tools to assist the learner. Most definitely, educational television can assist a local teacher by supplementing classroom instruction because it has the potential for opening a window to a world that would otherwise remain hidden from view. Television is a more expensive technology than radio at both the broadcast and reception locations.

Electronic files on magnetic or optical media can store large text, video, and audio files in relatively low-weight packages, thus reducing the cost of paper and shipping for the educational institution. A typical 3.5-inch formatted high-density computer floppy disk holds about 1.4 megabytes (MB) of data; for illustrative purposes, the word processor file for this chapter (20 double-spaced pages of typescript) occupies 110 kilobytes (0.11 MB) of disk space. Hence, 10 copies of the original file could be stored on one standard floppy. Disks recorded in IBM PC-compatible format are immediately readable by all standard personal computers equipped with floppy disk drives; disks recorded in Apple Macintosh format require "disk mounter" software to be read by IBM-compatible computers.

Just as there are duplicators for tapes, mass copying of floppy disks is now well developed. The decision to purchase disk-duplicating equipment versus contracting out the job largely depends on the volume of disks to be copied and the frequency of the need for duplication. Blank disks are relatively inexpensive and should be considered disposable items, that is, no effort should be made to recover them for distribution to another student or as a medium for storing newer files because repeated reading from and writing to the disk will ultimately lead to errors in the stored data. Floppy disks are not suitable for archival storage because the data can be easily destroyed by magnetic fields.

Large-capacity disks such as an Iomega Zip, Imation SuperDisk, or compatible suppliers afford storage in the range of 100 to 250 MB on a single disk. These disks are more expensive than the standard 1.4 MB floppies and require proprietary disk readers that are not standard equipment on most personal computers but are widely used and relatively inexpensive. (Several computer manufacturers now include an internal Zip disk drive as standard equipment on some models or as an option on others.)

A potential drawback to the use of these higher-capacity storage disks is the lack of readily available equipment for mass duplication, although in principle it should be possible to connect several of the drives to one computer to facilitate the copying process.

Compact discs (CDs) hold up to 650 MB of data. In addition to text and sound files, still pictures, animations, and movie and video clips are readily accommodated. Indeed, the large size of most video and audio files renders archiving them on 1.4 MB magnetic floppy disks impractical. Furthermore, CDs are cheaper than floppy disks per MB of storage space, have far longer useful lifetimes, and have low shipping and mailing costs because of their light weight. CD readers have long been standard equipment on all personal computers. Many newer models incorporate DVD readers, but these can read CDs as well.

Software (e.g., Adaptec's Toast) and drives for recording to CDs are reasonably priced, and some computer models now have these drives as standard equipment. Before writing to a CD (called "burning a disk"), all files must be in the desired final format. Unless the more expensive rewritable CDs are being used, errors can be corrected only by burning a new CD. Although the blank CDs are inexpensive, it takes about 20 minutes to copy the files to the CD. This becomes the original or master for making duplicates; any errors or imperfections on it will be reproduced faithfully on all copies.

Duplicating decks for making simultaneous multiple copies of CDs are not inexpensive but are certainly within a price range affordable for most educational institutions. Unless the program or institution routinely plans to make multiple CD copies and can allocate support staff to duplicating CDs, making and affixing labels, and inserting the finished CDs into protective covers, however, it probably makes more financial sense to contract these services to an outside vendor.

Increasingly, commercial textbooks are packaged with CD-ROMs containing supplemental materials, animations, video clips, and other extras. Instructors need to evaluate these materials to determine their accuracy and appropriateness for their course and clearly explain in the syllabus how these materials are to be used. It is particularly important to check that the instructions for using the CDs are correct and understandable for students. There is yet another reason for instructors to carefully peruse CDs that come with course textbooks—they may contain materials that save the instructor time!

The *Internet* refers to the globally interconnected series of smaller computer networks. The first demonstration of linking two computers across a long distance was achieved in 1965. By 1969, the first network (ARPANET) connecting four host computers in California and Utah was set up (Leiner et al., 2000).

Computers are networked when they are linked so that information can be passed from one computer to another or to a common-use printer, storage device, or other peripheral. For example, a small business occupying the 16th floor of a skyscraper may link its 10 desktop computers together in a loop to share electronic mail, facilitate file exchange, and access a shared printer. It is possible for one user on the network to read or write to the files on a coworker's computer. If the network is local, or self-contained, computers outside the small business office are not connected and cannot access the information on the company's computers, and the company's computers do not have access to electronic mail or information outside the office.

A local network usually contains a central host computer or server to which the other computers are linked, much as the spokes of a bicycle wheel are connected to the axle hub. The server contains a library of files that individual computers on the network can read, copy, or write to. Large applications, or programs, may reside on the server and receive instructions from and deliver results to a less powerful networked computer acting as a simple teletype terminal. In this type of network, information to be shared between two computers on the network must be passed from one computer to the central computer, which then routes the connection to the second networked computer.

An internet is created when gateways or routers are set up to connect different host computers. The connections may be by direct cable links, radio, microwave, or satellite. Today, Internet service providers (ISPs) are the routers of electronic traffic between the host computer at the center of each smaller network. Every server acts as a send-and-receive connection to an ISP. Just as each telephone account has a unique number, each network server has a unique numerical address to direct electronic traffic flow. Thus, the Internet is that combination of hardware and software necessary for the smooth exchange of electronic information between networks; by itself, the Internet is only a utility, much like phone service.

Originally, the Internet was limited to exchange of text and numerical data. Indeed, electronic mail (e-mail) was one of the earliest and most fruitful applications developed for use on the Internet, allowing researchers to rapidly exchange information. Even today, e-mail probably is the major use for the Internet. In the context of distance education, it represents the fastest and most inexpensive way for learner and instructor to remain in contact.

Early application programs for the Internet were command driven—that is, the operator had to learn specific code words that were entered by keyboard to effect the desired transfer. The development of Web browser programs such as NCSA Mosaic, Netscape Navigator, and Microsoft Internet Explorer, which incorporated menu-driven tools for reading text and viewing still images, making file transfers, sending e-mail, and conducting searches for information, enhanced the use and accessibility of the Internet. Specialized helper applications or plug-ins for Web browsers now allow automatic downloading and expansion of compressed files, execution of small programs or "applets"; viewing of objects in three dimensions; and transmission of both live and recorded video and audio, animations, and conferencing. The list of new tools seems to expand almost monthly.

A computer with an Internet connection and Web browser has become a multimedia presentation tool. The browser itself reads a hypertext markup language file (a text file ending in extensions such as .html or .htm) to obtain instructions for both the content and format of the page seen by the viewer. The HTML file may include references to other text, graphics, video, and sound files that are assembled into the final observed product page. Initially, the HTML files read by a browser had to be composed using a text or word processor by an operator knowledgeable in the syntax of the markup language. More recently, Web page composition programs incorporating graphical "point and click" interfaces have become commercially available, so that little or no formal knowledge of HTML programming code is required of the user. Both Web browsers themselves and recent versions of word processors include basic HTML composers. Although composition programs can speed the work of preparing Web pages, someone familiar with the current HTML standards is best suited to optimize them for final use and perform troubleshooting.

Web-based delivery of distance education has several advantages. For example, electronic files are more easily revised than paper documents and with essentially no waste; text, sound, and motion are readily combined to enhance the aesthetics of the learning experience; students have essentially on-demand access to course materials; widely dispersed resources can be accessed without travel; and the printing cost of documents is shifted from the institution to the student or the remote computer site. Web-based instruction, however, requires institutional expenditures for purchase and maintenance of servers, software and Web page development, user training, and fees for connection to ISPs. For learners, Web-based instruction (or other Internet-intensive methods) also requires ready access to computers, electricity, and a telephone system.

Not surprisingly, the expansion of distance education has both promoted and been assisted by the growth of businesses that develop software for delivery and management of Web-based courses. Products such as WebCT, Blackboard, Convene.com, and Academic.com provide templates that faculty or secretarial staff can use to publish their own course materials; the skill required to use these products is on the order of what is required to use a standard word processor. The products usually integrate other features such as chat, bulletin boards, whiteboards, online quizzing, and so forth. The company may host the courseware on its own servers. Other commercial products provide course content that can be customized by the faculty member; Archipelago is one representative of this class of product. We will have further comments on this subject in Chapter 6.

Listservers, bulletin boards or discussion groups, chat rooms, whiteboards, and conferencing software are more recent communication applications transmitted via the Internet. Chat rooms, whiteboards, and conferencing were described earlier under synchronous methods of delivery.

Listservers, or *listservs,* are mass e-mail programs designed to serve an audience with a specific common interest. For example, an active listserv for those interested in distance education, the Distance Education Online Symposium (DEOS), is hosted at Pennsylvania State University.[1] An individual joins the mail group of interest by sending a "subscribe to list" command to the host server, which in turn adds the subscriber's e-mail address to the list of recipients. When any member sends a message to the listserv, it is an open communication automatically forwarded to all members of the group. The subject of the message and a date and time stamp are usually included with the mail. In turn, recipients have the choice of replying to the sending author only or to all the members of the list, saving the message, or deleting it. Depending on the activity and size of the group, members can receive a few to hundreds of e-mails a day. Although communication is asynchronous, a lively discussion can nonetheless take place amid rapid-fire exchange of messages and replies before the group exhausts the topic. Usually, several topics are discussed at the same time—this is why the subject header in the e-mail becomes important. The header provides a connection or "thread" that a member of the list can follow while selecting messages to read to maintain a sense of continuity. Some groups offer members the option of receiving all the messages bundled together in one large mailing or digest. Listservs may afford subscribers the option to temporarily suspend receipt of messages; other group mail lists maintain an archive of past postings, often searchable according to the topic.

Bulletin boards or *discussion groups* have a purpose similar to listservs but differ in how the information is disseminated publicly. Listservs are like mass postal mailings—messages are sent indiscriminately to every mailbox on the route; the recipient is obliged to receive the mail but may discard it. An electronic bulletin board is like the physical posting boards found in grocery stores and student unions: Messages are tacked in open view for any passerby who cares to stop and peruse them. Thus, an electronic bulletin board is a site that must be accessed through the Internet. A message sent to the site is published there, showing the subject, date and time of posting, and the author's name or pseudonym. Access to the bulletin board can be limited by passwords issued to authorized users. Depending on the sophistication of the software, archiving, sorting, and searching of postings may be possible.

Conclusion

We have briefly described the wide array of methods commonly used to disseminate course content and maintain interaction between the instructor and student in distance education. There is no one ideal technology for delivering course content or maintaining contact, nor can a single method fulfill all the educational needs of a distance education program. Hence, this chapter has been directed toward providing readers with at least a superficial familiarity with the various types of technology available as a prelude to choosing the particular methods employed to implement a distance program. Tables 5.1, 5.2, and 5.3 summarize our presentation. The next chapter examines the principles that guide the selection of the delivery methods for distance education courses.

WWw ➤   At our Sage Web site, www.sagepub.com/mehrotra

Visit our companion Web site to find

- Links to vendors of the commercial products mentioned in this chapter
- More background information on methods for delivering course content in distance education programs
- Links to sites demonstrating or using Internet technologies in distance education
- Tips on designing user-friendly cross-platform Web pages for distance education courses

TABLE 5.1 Summary of Synchronous Delivery Methods for Distance
Education

Method	Strengths	Weaknesses
Interactive television (ITV)	Mimics sense of traditional class environment	Expensive hardware
Telephone: Conversation	• Established technology • Personalized attention possible	• One-on-one nature limits number of contacts per instructor • Conference calls limit personalized attention
Internet conferencing: Audio	• May avoid long-distance toll charges • Multiple tools can be used concurrently	Sound may be of poorer quality than telephone
Internet conferencing: Video and audio	• Less expensive than ITV • Multiple tools can be used concurrently	• Video files are large • Current bandwidth inadequate • Motion is not smooth • Sound and motion not synchronized well
Internet conferencing: Chat	• Rapid communication • May involve many participants • Session can be archived	Few
Internet conferencing: Whiteboard	• Rapid sharing of graphical information • Session can be archived	Few

TABLE 5.2 Summary of Asynchronous Delivery Methods for
Distance Education

Method	Strengths	Weaknesses
Print (paper)	• Low cost • Students do not need to learn how to use a new technology • Students can submit work in same format	• Bulky materials • Slow transfer rate
Audiocassette	• Established technology • Inexpensive, reusable medium • Students can submit work in same format	• Sound needs to be supplemented with written or visual materials
Telephone: Answering machine	• Established technology • Automated • Round-the-clock access possible	• Limited scope • Interactive systems expensive
Telephone: Facsimile (fax) machine	• Established technology • Rapid, automated transfer of documents possible • Can be used by students to submit work	• Time-consuming for many contacts • Paper supply must be monitored
Videocassette	• Pervasive technology • Students can submit work in same medium	• More expensive to produce than audiocassettes • Students may have limited access to recording cameras

TABLE 5.2 (Continued)

Method	Strengths	Weaknesses
Radio broadcast	• Low technological demand on user side • Inexpensive and pervasive technology for reception • Mass coverage possible	• Same medium cannot be used by student to submit work • Individualized instruction is not possible
Television broadcast	• Visuals and sound reinforce each other • Mass coverage, yet each student has "close-up" view	• Expensive technology on broadcast side • No individualized instruction • Same medium cannot be used by student to submit work
Electronic files: Magneto-optical storage	• Low cost, easy to revise • Little space required for storage • Students can use same medium for submission of work	• Fragility, short lifetime of magnetic media
Electronic mail: E-mail	• Widely available • Already familiar technology to many students • Rapid exchange of messages possible • Students can receive and submit assignments	• Not all e-mail programs allow attachment of document files • Can be time-consuming for instructor to read and respond to messages

NOTE: Table 5.3 summarizes Web-based asynchronous methods.

TABLE 5.3 Summary of Web-Based Asynchronous Delivery
Methods for Distance Education

Method	Strengths	Weaknesses
Web pages	• Can combine text, graphics, and audio-visual files • Rapidly and easily updated	• Time and skill needed to compose Web documents • Web pages may not appear the same on all computers or in all Web browsers
File transfer	• Most Web browsers automate file transfer • Compressed files are transferred quickly • Faster than mailing paper documents	• Unless files are in portable document format (.pdf), students need the same software used to compose document or a translator
Audio	• A separate playback device is not needed • Sound files can be integrated with text and picture files	• Quality of the sound variable
Video	• Videocassette player and television not needed • Video files can be integrated with sound, text, and picture files.	• Large file size • Quality poorer than video-cassette

TABLE 5.3 (Continued)

Method	Strengths	Weaknesses
Animation/ movies	• Files often smaller and better quality than video	• Large time investment to make animations or movies • Files may be large
Bulletin boards	• Discussions can be accomplished flexibly, does not require all participants to be on-line at same time • Discussion can be reviewed at later date by instructor or students	• Few • Password protection for access may be required to preclude vandals from making postings • Proper "netiquette" must be enforced by instructor
Comprehensive commercial packages (e.g., WebCT, Blackboard)	• Many desired functions provided in one program • Template-based design requires no programming skills • Technical support available to students and faculty • Lower investment in computer hardware if vendor hosts course materials	• All features in package may not be needed for the program • Some desired features may not be provided by the package

Note

1. Distance Education Online Symposium (DEOS) listserv: Send an e-mail to listserv@lists.psu.edu; in the reference line, type "subscribe DEOS-L"; in the e-mail message area, simply type "subscribe DEOS-your name." You may also subscribe separately to the electronic newsletter on distance education, DEOS-News. Send your e-mail to the same address as the listserv but with the message "subscribe DEOS-NEWS your name." Be sure to send the message from the e-mail account at which you wish to receive postings and newsletters from the server.

References

Borland, J. (1999). *Programmers prepare free, new MP3 format* [Online]. Retrieved June 16, 2000, from the World Wide Web: www.canada.cnet.com/news/0-1005-200-2091466.html

Carr, S. (2000, March 24). Even public speaking can be taught online. *Chronicle of Higher Education, 46*, A46. Retrieved April 9, 2001, from the World Wide Web: www. chronicle.com/chronicle/archive.htm

DiPaolo, A. (1999, December). Stanford learning: Worldwide availability on-demand at Stanford online. *Technological Horizons in Education Journal, 27*(5), 16-18.

FJM Multimedia Inc. (1999). *World television standards* [Online]. Retrieved April 8, 2001, from the World Wide Web: www.fjm-media.com/worldtv.htm

Leiner, B. M., Cerf, V. G., Clark, D. D., Kahn, R. E., Kleinrock, L., Lynch, D. C., Postel, J., Roberts, L. G., & Wolff, S. (2000). *A brief history of the Internet.* [Online]. Reston, VA: Internet Society. Retrieved April 8, 2001, from the World Wide Web: www.isoc.org/internet-history/brief.html

Rodes, P., Knapczyk, D., Chapman, C., & Chung, H. (2000, December). Involving teachers in Web-based professional development. *Technological Horizons in Education Journal, 27*(10), 94-102.

Young, J. R. (2000a, May 12). The lowly telephone is central to some distance-education courses [Online]. *Chronicle of Higher Education, 46*, A46. Retrieved April 9, 2001, from the World Wide Web: www.chronicle.com/chronicle/archive.htm

Young, J. R. (2000b, July 7). Moving the seminar table to the computer screen [Online]. *Chronicle of Higher Education, 46*, A33. Retrieved April 9, 2001, from the World Wide Web: www.chronicle.com/chronicle/archive.htm

6

Selecting Delivery Methods

Let us now imagine that the educational institution has made the strategic decision to offer a program wholly or partly by distance learning. Once the specific courses to be offered by distance delivery have been identified, how should the delivery methods be selected? We have deliberately chosen the plural form *methods* in asking this question: It is unlikely that a single technology or delivery method can fulfill all the educational objectives successfully, and it certainly would be a mistake to assume so from the outset of program or course planning. Given the large variety of methods from which to choose, the momentary popularity of one method over another, the competition between educational and economic objectives, and the usual urgency to "get on with the job" under time constraints, there is a great temptation to choose delivery methods hastily and for the wrong reasons. The consequences of making poor choices of delivery methods may include an educationally inferior experience for students and faculty alike, lost revenue for the institution, and expensive tweaking during the program's course—or even worse, a need to completely overhaul the program.

In this chapter, we propose several principles that should guide the choice of distance education delivery methods—principles derived from good practices for distance education (Chapter 3), our experience, and observation. After elaborating on these guiding points, we offer a decision tree or rubric constructed on these principles that readers can use to arrive at a choice of delivery methods for their particular programs.

Fundamental Principles to Observe in Selecting Delivery Methods

On the basis of observation and experience, we have arrived at several basic principles we adhere to in choosing delivery methods for distance learning.

> A. *First, identify the teaching or learning objectives to be achieved, and then choose the technology tools that make the goals achievable.*

This is the first and most important principle. Violate it at your own peril!

At the program level, the sponsoring institution must have established a clear set of outcomes in knowledge, practice, and attitude for its graduates before launching program delivery at a distance. If the program is an existing one offered in traditional on-campus format, these outcomes should already exist, although perhaps they have not been formally identified previously. Programs that undergo periodic review for accreditation undoubtedly will have confronted this issue already (Chapter 11). Once these program outcomes have been identified, the next step is to determine what specific outcomes are to be fulfilled by particular course offerings. For example, attainment of core knowledge in the discipline often can be distributed among courses that address specific subdisciplines. Some topics may be treated exclusively within a single course, whereas others are covered from different perspectives in multiple courses. The result of any such analysis should be a detailed list identifying what objectives a course in the program is intended to accomplish and how these mesh with the other courses in the program. The process we have just described is an essential prelude to choosing delivery methods but should not seem to be an unusual or excessive exercise: It is standard good educational practice and works hand in hand with assessment of learning outcomes (Chapter 9) and program evaluation (Chapter 10).

Having identified the objectives for a course, the instructional team has completed about one half the work needed to choose delivery methods wisely. From this point, the task becomes one of matching the educational objectives to compatible delivery methods that are practical within the context of the institution's financial concerns.

Imagine a course that has as one objective teaching students the art of weaving willow baskets. Knowing this, certain delivery methods can be rejected outright as poor choices. Thus, any technique using only sound, such as audiocassette, radio broadcast, or telephone call, would be inappropriate. Without visual aids, the task of learning to weave is far more inefficient and frustrating than it should be. Even if the coaching is delivered synchronously (Chapter 5), both teacher and student are hampered by lack of visual clues. In a similar vein, a course attempting to teach conversational French is doomed if it lacks a component supporting sound. Text with pronunciation marks and pictures of how the mouth should be shaped to say *"Comment allez vous?"* are in no way a substitute for hearing the phrase properly enunciated.

Our second principle is a corollary to the first.

B. Subordinate technology to the educational objectives.

Another way to phrase this principle might be this: Do not choose a technology tool simply because it is "cool" or has a high "gee-whiz" factor.

Imagine an introduction to accounting course delivered via the Internet. Words or graphics can be designed as links associated with sound files, animations, and video clips. All these enhancements may be valuable on commercial sites or those providing entertainment, but on pages dedicated to teaching accounting, they become distractions unless used judiciously. For example, an interactive lesson leading students through the steps needed to prepare a monthly financial statement for a small business may be significantly enhanced with some carefully chosen animated pointers or fades between views of a ledger. A sweeping orchestral score or an animation of a rabbit in an accountant's visor running around with a red pen may show the page composer's skill as a programmer but not as an educator.

Different technologies may support the same educational objective. For example, in teaching a foreign language, auditory clues obviously are important to assist the learner in speaking another tongue understandably. The student could hear the lesson by means of ITV, an audiocassette, an audio file on a CD, a phone call to a recorded message, or downloading a sound file from the Internet, and so on. Each of these methods accomplishes delivery of the pronunciation lesson, but only ITV allows synchronous interaction between student and teacher. The other methods alone do not afford the student the means to provide a sample of his or her pronunciation for evaluation and correction. If evaluation of the student's language skills are handled by another technology, then the combined asynchronous methods are certainly cheaper delivery and evaluation modes than is ITV. Still, the student will not receive immediate feedback unless ITV is the technology of choice. Thus, the program managers and instructors must decide whether the educational value of immediate feedback provided by ITV is necessary and affordable in the context of their institution's goals and financial circumstances.

C. Choose technologies that are appropriate to the educational, geographic, social, and economic status of learners.

Another way of phrasing this principle might be this: Avoid the one-size-fits-all mentality of delivery. Entirely different modes of delivery may be needed to achieve the same outcomes in the same course delivered to different populations.

Imagine a distance history course about the role of the United States in the Second World War. The course is to be offered to several target groups: urban adults aged 25 to 35 years who work during the day; retired older citizens living in their own homes; and Native Americans aged 25 to 35 years living on a remote reservation noted for its general level of poverty. The content of the course has already been selected to speak to issues of interest to all three segments of the student population. The three groups differ in their access to technology for delivery of the course and in their comfort level with the delivery technology.

Prior to developing the course, the institution carried out a marketing and needs assessment of the target student groups and found the following: The urban young adults prefer to take a course delivered through the Internet because that allows them the flexibility of studying at odd hours. The group of older retired students includes some avid computer user-owners, but most learners in this group have little knowledge of or access to personal computers with Internet connections. Members of the largest subgroup prefer to watch videotaped presentations at their own time and pace. On this particular reservation, many homes lack electricity and hence have no television or computers. The reservation community center is equipped with large-screen televisions with cassette players for group viewing and receives most programming by satellite dish.

Armed with the preceding information, the school decided to package the course in video format supplemented by printed course workbooks for the older adult and Native American students and as a Web-based course for the urban students. The printed course materials were the same for all students, although in electronic form for the Web-based delivery. Instead of the "talking heads" and moving pictures of the video, the Web format included the text of the video narrative, illustrative still photos taken from the video, and a few audio clips. The urban students were also given the option of using the video format of the course.

In this scenario, more effort was required to develop two delivery modes, but in doing so, the sponsoring institution benefits from having a larger pool of students to whom the course could be marketed.

The next principle is similar to the previous one.

D. Use a delivery mode as transparently as possible.

Students should be able to focus their time and energy on the course's educational content, not on receiving it. This is called *transparent delivery*. Little good is accomplished in selecting a delivery method compatible with course objectives and the socioeconomic characteristics of the learners if avoidable technical difficulties distract students from their studies or cause frustration. Students need training and support in using the delivery technology for the course. Content delivery should use the least obtrusive technology. As many procedures as practical should be automated. When students must execute certain specific operations, they should be provided step-by-step reminders at the appropriate points.

Here are some examples of making course delivery transparent:

1. All custom-printed workbooks and study guides should be paginated, should include tables of contents, and should be cross-referenced in correct chronological sequence in the syllabus, just as a commercially available textbook is referenced (see Chapter 4).

2. When ITV is the delivery method, make sure that the camera remains focused on the speaker or materials on the blackboard. Do not obstruct students' line of sight. Ensure that all microphones are operating properly before class begins. Have a technician standing by at each ITV node during the class period so that problems can be fixed immediately. Faculty should practice (yes!) their television presentation skills in an attempt to eliminate personal habits or mannerisms on-screen that are distracting to students. ITV faculty also need to avoid unnecessary movements that cannot be smoothly tracked by the camera.

3. Clearly label audio- or videocassettes, CDs, floppy disks, and so on to indicate what they contain and in what order they are used in the course. Also, provide a schedule (ideally in the syllabus) showing the chronological order in which the materials are used in the course.

4. Construct Web pages so that navigation is clear. Users should be able to know where they are within the site and how to go from one point to another. This can be accomplished best by displaying a menu on every page or at the least by including a site map. Minimize jumps from within the body of a document to external sites or other pages within the site. Use "Web safe" colors chosen from a standard palette that will be rendered the same way by different browsers, computer operating systems, and monitors. Test all pages on several computer platforms before loading them on the server. Keep picture files as small as possible; a good strategy is to use thumbnail pictures that download rapidly with the page. Use these small snapshots as links to enlarged versions that students may elect to download. Large downloadable files should be stored in portable document format (.pdf) and compressed for transfer. If the site makes use of any plug-ins or helper applications that are not standard components of the Web browser, provide links to the source of these programs.

Students taking distance learning courses are often busy people. As consumers, they will appreciate having class materials presented in a fashion that allows them to spend the maximum time studying, learning, and completing course assignments. The likelihood of students successfully attaining course learning outcomes will be increased by transparent delivery, which allows them to stay focused on the course content.

E. Devise alternate delivery methods for students having special needs.

The term *special needs* connotes two things in the present context. The first concerns those students lacking access to some element of technology used for course delivery. Consider students living in rural areas who must use a long-distance dial-up to connect with an Internet service provider (ISP). If the course or program in which they wish to enroll is largely Web based in its delivery, the extra toll charges may dissuade them from pursuing their studies. This problem can be remedied fairly easily, however, if most of the course content is hosted by the university's own server: The needed files can be copied to a CD-ROM disk and mailed to the student. At home, the Web browser can be used in offline mode, that is, not connected to the ISP, to read the files directly from the CD. For quicker access, the files can be transferred to the student's computer hard disk drive. One reminder: If copyright permissions have been secured for any course materials, make sure that the permission covers the transfer of data to the CD.

The second sense of *special needs* refers to students requiring accommodations because of a health-related or physical condition. As we note in Chapter 7, the Americans With Disabilities Act of 1990 requires that reasonable accommodations be afforded to students having documented physical limitations. By and large, each student's situation must be addressed on a case-by-case basis, but a certain amount of creative thought will provide some possible solutions. For example, a student having impaired vision may well be able to pursue studies through Web-based instruction more readily than in traditional textbook format simply because the font type and size of text, as well as the resolution of computer monitors, can be changed easily at the student's end. The distance education program may need to help the student make the adjustments in the formatting menus in software or control panels in the computer hardware. Indeed, distance course methods may appropriately accommodate some students who have difficulty succeeding in the traditional classroom. A student suffering comprehension difficulties that make note taking difficult in a typical campus lecture may find a Web-based or video-based course more satisfactory and less frustrating because it is compatible with working at a slower pace as well as affording instant replay of any difficult moments in the class presentation.

Principles A through E that we have just discussed emphasize aspects of choosing delivery methods that most immediately affect students. We now mention three principles that more directly affect the instructor and institution.

F. Choose technologies that are established, reliable, adaptable to a range of disciplines, and well supported.

Many persons have had the experience of rushing out to buy the "latest and greatest" thing only to find that the shiny new model car, computer, or software has a few kinks in it that the manufacturer had not completely dealt with before bringing the product to market. Why should the technology and tools for distance education be any different? It is especially important for an institution making its initial foray into distance education to allocate resources wisely because start-up costs of some technologies (such as ITV) are quite high.

Employing a consistent delivery method for as many courses within a program as is appropriate makes sense on several levels. Both students and faculty will become more adept at using the technology, requiring less training during the program, and the delivery should become more transparent with repeated use. In addition, as more courses use the same delivery method, some economies of scale may result, reducing the delivery cost per student.

Technical support for students in distance education courses is essential, although the college or university offering the distance program need not be solely responsible for all such support. Thus, fixes for problems such as replacement of defective copies of tapes and disks or lost passwords for logging on to the campus computer network should be handled readily enough by the home institution's support services. When commercial products are being used in the distance program, support can be approached in several ways. Most software programs have built-in help functions that are quite good; Web browsers such as Netscape and Internet Explorer are two prominent examples. A good strategy in providing support is to first make students in the course or program aware of the resources immediately available to them. Many problems can be resolved at that level, and if some seem to arise more frequently than others, a list of common problems and how to fix them can be prepared for students to access. For difficulties still not resolved by the student with the assistance already provided, the institution needs to decide whether to provide the help or redirect the student to the supplier. In selecting any software or hardware for delivery, we suggest a careful evaluation of the quality of the instructions that come with the product and the assistance that is later available from the manufacturer. Before the course begins, the institution should decide what types and level of support to provide and set up the mechanism for supplying the support. Students will become frustrated if the delivery method impedes the learning experience; that frustration is greatly relieved by making appropriate technical support available. If it is not, student dissatisfaction may translate into poor retention.

G. Make plans for an alternate delivery scheme that can be deployed rapidly if the primary delivery system fails ("crashes").

Educational institutions are not exempt from Murphy's Law. Try to imagine realistic scenarios for interruption of course delivery, and make plans for providing alternate service to students. For example, if the program uses Web-based methods, consider dealing with a server crash. A possible solution: Have a mirror site (an alternate server, either on campus or an outside vendor) to which traffic can be redirected. It is common practice to keep backup tapes of files on hand for rapidly reloading servers should that be needed. If ITV service may be interrupted for a substantial period, consider making agreements in advance for alternate carriers, or if that is not feasible, have prerecorded videotaped sessions. If the synchronous aspect of the class is the more important element, consider conducting class by speaker phone for two-way communication, with visual aids being sent by fax to the remote site for use during the phone conversation. Clearly, every contingency cannot be foreseen or corrected. It may be preferable to have assignments held in reserve for students to pursue on their own in such cases.

H. *Choose delivery methods that maximize the time that instructors can spend assisting students.*

A common but mistaken notion is that distance education courses require less faculty attention than traditional on-campus courses, and certainly it is possible to design the course with this objective in mind. The situation is not much different in some respects from offering a lecture class with an enrollment of 500 students. It is also equally true that some subjects are not amenable to being taught this way and require more frequent interaction between teacher and learner. As we described in "Good Practices in Distance Education" (Chapter 3), student attainment of learning objectives is generally enhanced by frequent contact with and feedback from instructors.

Accomplishing the goal of frequent teacher-student interaction in distance learning means that the faculty member should not be primarily responsible for maintaining the technology of delivery. This implies the existence of support personnel. The level of technical support available to the teaching faculty has a direct bearing on the time that can be dedicated to student-teacher interaction. For example, programs making use of audio- or videotapes require support staff to control cameras and audio and lighting levels, duplicate and label tapes, and manage the flow of the tapes to and from students. It is a poor use of resources to have a faculty member running or supervising the duplication of tapes. If the program plans to use audio- or videocassettes and a full-time support staff is not financially possible, the institution needs to examine what work can be done by unskilled part-time labor and what services must be contracted with an outside vendor.

As another example, consider Web-based courses. The faculty member's primary responsibility should be determining course content, assisting students, and evaluating their progress. Converting course content to Web format may be assigned to the faculty member as well, although not all faculty possess the skill to do so. If the size of the institution's technology support staff is too small or cannot grow to serve all the faculty involved in Web-based courses, it probably makes sense for the institution to contract the services of an external vendor supplying Internet course delivery packages. Products such as WebCT, Convene.com, and Academic.com provide templates that faculty or secretarial staff can use to enter their own materials. The skill required to use these products is similar to that needed to use a standard word processor. Other commercial offerings provide course content that can be customized by the instructors; Archipelago is a company known for this type of service.

Finally, the choice of delivery method, the number and type of faculty-student interactions per term, and the length of each interaction must be carefully considered in setting enrollment limits for the course. Thus, a course in which students log on to a discussion board to converse with the professor is consistent with a higher enrollment than a course in which one-on-one interaction is required.

A Decision Tree Approach
to Selecting a Delivery Method

The choice of the delivery method to be used for a distance education course or program is not simply an educational one but also a financial one dependent on the resources the institution can commit to such a program and its expectations for generating revenue from the program. These policy issues cannot be addressed here.

In this section, we provide a step-by-step guide for selecting delivery methods based on the technical capabilities of each method. Before this decision tree is used, the program should have already identified the educational objectives for a particular course.

Like any decision tree, ours asks a question at each step and uses the response to direct the user to the next question, and so on, each step narrowing the range of possibilities. We have arranged the process in two formats, one text-based, and the other graphical (see figures at the end of the chapter). Please refer to Chapter 5 for descriptions of the technologies mentioned below.

OPENING QUESTION

Question 1: Do your educational objectives require live or real-time instruction?

Yes: Synchronous delivery methods are needed. Go to Section 1, "Synchronous Delivery."

No: Asynchronous delivery may be employed. Go to Section 2, "Asynchronous Delivery."

SECTION 1: SYNCHRONOUS DELIVERY

Question 1.1: Do you need visual and voice interaction between instructors and students, as in a seminar or language class in an on-campus classroom?

Yes: Consider using interactive television (ITV).
No: Go to the next question.

Question 1.2: Is it more important that students see and hear course content live than interact with the instructor? This is much like having a lecture-only class.

Yes: ITV can be used if students all gather in the same location. If students do not gather, consider a live streaming video/audio broadcast via the Internet ("Netcasts") or educational television broadcast.
No: Go to the next question.

Question 1.3: Is live audio delivery alone adequate for your purposes?
Yes:
1. Consider a telephone conference link-up to a remote site if significant numbers of students are involved and if two-way communication is needed, or consider a conference call to several telephone numbers if few students are involved.
2. Consider a live streaming audio broadcast via the Internet if students are not gathering in common.
3. Consider a live radio broadcast if students do not have access to Internet connections.

Question 1.4: Are text-based methods (with or without graphics) adequate for your purposes?
Yes:
1. If no graphics need to be consulted during the class period, consider setting up an Internet chat room that students must log on to at a specific day and time.
2. If graphics are needed in addition to text chat, try using a Web-based conferencing application such as Netscape's Conference.

SECTION 2: ASYNCHRONOUS DELIVERY

Question 2.1: Will any computer-based technology be used to deliver course content?

Yes: Go to Question 2.3.
No: Go to Question 2.2.

Question 2.2: Will you make video or audio presentations?

Yes:

1. Consider videocassette recordings for video-with-audio or video only, digital videodiscs (DVD), or movie reels (nearly obsolete).
2. Audio-only content can be delivered on audiocassette tapes, CD-ROM disks, magnetic tape reels (nearly obsolete), or phonograph records (nearly obsolete).

No: The remaining asynchronous methods are print based.

Commercial textbooks, or those materials published in-house such as manuals, readers, study guides, pamphlets, charts, diagrams, and so on: All printed materials described must be delivered to students by postal or package delivery services. Facsimile transfer via phone lines is feasible only for short printed items sent to a limited number of students.

Question 2.3: Do the computer-based methods include Internet- or Web-based delivery? Note: Electronic mail (e-mail) only is not included here.

Yes: Go to Question 2.5.

No: Go to Question 2.4.

Question 2.4: Are you planning to use e-mail to deliver course content?

Yes: E-mail has some drawbacks for delivery of course content. Formatted files are normally transferred as an attachment to the e-mail message. Some e-mail programs or service providers (AOL comes to mind), however, either are not compatible with attachments or do not reliably transfer the files intact. E-mail is best used for communicating messages. If reliable file transfer is desired, specify what programs and/or service providers students should use.

No: If the Internet is not being used for computer-based course content delivery, this implies that students will be receiving files by mail for the course for use on their local computer. The files or programs can be stored on floppy disks, high-capacity storage disks (such as Zip or Jaz), or optical disks (CD-ROM). Make sure file types are compatible with each student's computer system and software.

Question 2.5: Do you plan to use the Internet only as a means for students to transfer or download files for use on their local computer?

Yes: All you need is a file transfer protocol (FTP) site, and students need FTP applications such as Dartmouth College's "Fetch."

Although this approach does not require a Web browser, it is now more common to incorporate downloadable files into Web pages because the transfer is automated.

No: This implies that the Internet delivery will be Web based, that students will work through a browser such as Netscape or Microsoft's Internet Explorer.

Question 2.6: Will Web pages for your program be constructed by individuals with experience writing HTML code?

Yes: The Web designer can use a text editor, HTML editor, or Web page composition program.

No: The author should use a Web page composition program such as Macromedia Dreamweaver, Allaire HomeSite, or Microsoft FrontPage. Guidance from an experienced Web page designer is also advisable.

Question 2.7: Will your Web pages include static pictures or graphics?

Yes: You will need image converter programs to save photographs and line drawings in joint photographic experts group format (.jpeg or .jpg), graphic interchange format (.gif), tagged image file format (.tiff), and related formats.

Question 2.8: Will students download files from your Web pages?

Yes: Use file compression programs such as Aladdin Systems Stuffit Deluxe to increase the rate of transfer.

Question 2.9: Will your Web pages include downloadable files that can be opened without access to the program creating them?

Yes: Software for creating portable document files (.pdf format) is needed, for example, Adobe Acrobat.

Question 2.10: Will Web pages include animations or movies?

Yes: Animated *gifs* (a series of still pictures played in rapid sequence) do not require plug-ins. More sophisticated vector-based animations in proprietary formats such as Macromedia Shockwave Flash (.swf) or Apple QuickTime require a plug-in for the viewer's browser. Of course, specialized software also is needed to generate the animation.

Question 2.11: Will video or audio clips be part of your Web pages?

Yes: Use streaming delivery to make transfer as rapid as possible. Avoid older formats that require the entire file to transfer before play begins. The student's browser must have the appropriate plug-in.

OTHER ISSUES

Question 2.12: Will your course include online discussions that do not require graphics?

Yes: Use bulletin board software for students to post comments and replies. (Synchronous discussion requires chat room software.)

Question 2.13: Will discussions require that graphics be included?

Yes: Use whiteboard software.

Question 2.14: Do you expect to incorporate online quizzes or tests into your program?

Yes: Several strategies are available:
1. Use a commercial product such as WebCT that incorporates tools for constructing, administering, and scoring tests online.
2. Secure the services of a testing company such as Prometric Computer Testing Centers.
3. Employ an experienced programmer to write the scripts needed for managing testing from your institution's server.

Conclusion

Selecting the most appropriate delivery methods for distance education begins with identifying the desired educational outcomes and objectives for the course or program. Often, different technologies may be used to attain the same desired outcomes. Which delivery method constitutes the "correct" choice depends on the characteristics of the student population being served, the host institution's financial concerns and resource limitations, and the purely academic goals already identified. The interplay among these concerns is complex and unique to each institution. We have offered several guiding principles and provided a decision tree to facilitate the selection process facing faculty and administrators of distance education programs (see Figures 6.1 through 6.5).

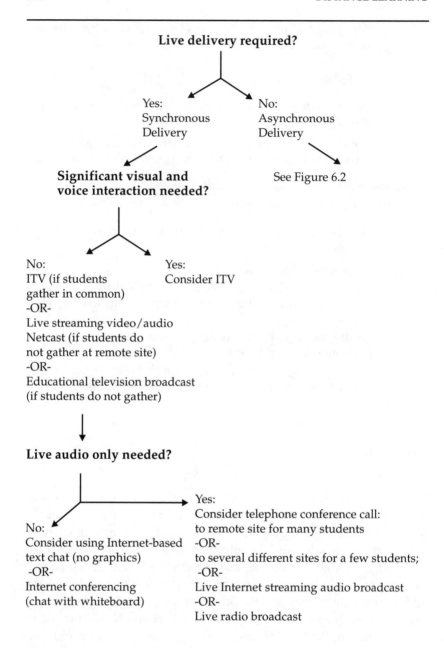

Figure 6.1. Graphical Decision Tree for Selecting Synchronous Delivery Methods

Are computer-based delivery methods being used?

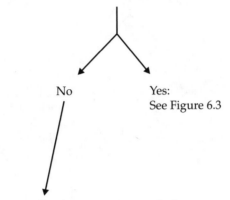

No

Yes:
See Figure 6.3

Are video or audio presentations needed?

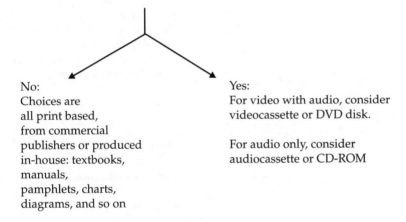

No:
Choices are
all print based,
from commercial
publishers or produced
in-house: textbooks,
manuals,
pamphlets, charts,
diagrams, and so on

Yes:
For video with audio, consider
videocassette or DVD disk.

For audio only, consider
audiocassette or CD-ROM

Figure 6.2. Graphical Decision Tree for Selecting Asynchronous Delivery
Methods Not Requiring Computers

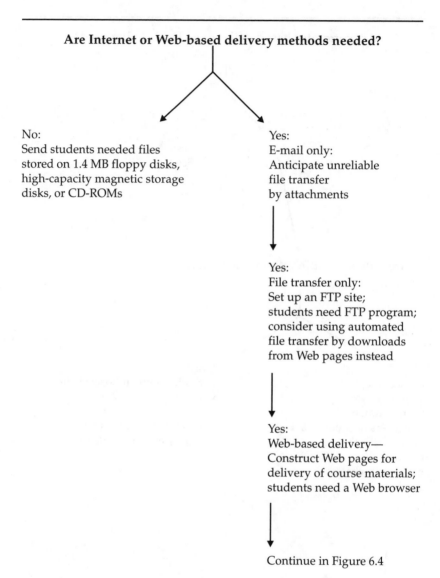

Are Internet or Web-based delivery methods needed?

No:
Send students needed files
stored on 1.4 MB floppy disks,
high-capacity magnetic storage
disks, or CD-ROMs

Yes:
E-mail only:
Anticipate unreliable
file transfer
by attachments

Yes:
File transfer only:
Set up an FTP site;
students need FTP program;
consider using automated
file transfer by downloads
from Web pages instead

Yes:
Web-based delivery—
Construct Web pages for
delivery of course materials;
students need a Web browser

Continue in Figure 6.4

Figure 6.3. Graphical Decision Tree for Selecting Asynchronous Delivery
Methods Requiring Computers

Will an experienced Web designer prepare course Web pages?

No:
Use a Web site construction
program; consult with
experienced programmer
as required

Yes:
Use a text or HTML editor,
or use a Web page
composing program and
tweak code as needed

If Web pages are to contain:
Static graphics
Downloadable files
Portable documents
Animations

Video and/or audio

Then these tools will be needed:
Image file converters
Compression for large files
A PDF generator program
Composing software and
    browser plug-ins for viewing
Streaming software and
    browser plug-ins

Figure 6.4. Graphical Decision Tree for Selecting Asynchronous, Web-Based
Delivery Methods

Other Issues

If you plan to use
Online discussion without graphics
Online discussion with graphics
Online testing

Integrated course management software

Then these tools are needed:
Bulletin board software
Chat and whiteboard software
Code-writing skills or software
    vendor
Commercial product

Figure 6.5. Other Issues to Consider in Selecting Asynchronous, Internet- or
Web-Based Delivery Methods

WWw ▶ At our Sage Web site, www.sagepub.com/mehrotra

Visit our Web site to find links to vendors for the products mentioned in this chapter and links to sites demonstrating or using the technologies we have discussed.

7

Support Services

Student support is an essential element of teaching and learning, and it is of critical importance in distance learning (Phipps, Wellman, & Merisotis, 1998). In addition, accrediting bodies are concerned about the quality of support services to distance learners and can be expected to carefully examine the areas of admissions, financial aid, academic advising, delivery of course materials, and placement and counseling (see Chapter 11). In this chapter, we define *support services* broadly to include virtually all the institution's interactions with students except those conveying instructional content. Distance students need almost the same services as do resident students, but traveling to campus is inconvenient and often not feasible. The challenge is to find ways to deliver the support services at a distance, just as instruction is delivered at a distance. Developing the capacity to deliver support services at a distance often has a double payoff: It helps attract and retain distance learners, and it can markedly increase convenience and efficiency for an institution's resident students, for example, by enabling online admissions and registration systems for all students.

Continuing advances in technology have made the Internet a versatile tool for support services, as have advances in the use of automated telephone information systems. Although institutions have harnessed both of these to provide high-quality support services, we will focus primarily on the use of the World Wide Web to deliver support services. In developing Web-based support services, readers will also find it helpful to consult the *Guide to Developing Online Student Services*, developed by Barbara Krauth and Jennifer Carbajal (2000) and posted for a limited time on the Web site of the Western Interstate Commission for Higher Education (WICHE).[1] It provides samples of Web pages of higher education institutions in the West and Midwest that exemplified good practices in student support services at the time of the study. Readers may also find it helpful to peruse at the same Web site a related report by Dirr (1999) of a survey of 417 higher education institutions' practices in providing support services to distance learners.

Providing support services to distance learners begins as the program recruits students; continues while the students are enrolled; and extends even beyond graduation to services for alumni, such as career counseling and job placement. We will examine support services for distance students in all three phases.

Before enrollment:

- Information to prospective students

- Admissions

- Financial aid

- Academic advising

- Registration

While enrolled:

- Bookstore services

- Library services

- Technical support

- Tutoring

- Services for students with disabilities

After course or program completion:

- Transcript service
- Alumni associations
- Continuing education opportunities
- Career services

One key principle is relevant to all the above support areas: Make the medium providing the services as user-friendly as possible, to enable distance learners to do as much business as possible. The following suggestions should be kept in mind in developing Web pages for support services:

- Create a distance learning page and provide a prominent link to it on the institution's home page and on other key Web pages of the institution. See, for example, the University of Washington Web page.[2]

- Create a menu on the distance course or program home page with links to each of the support services, and show the menu on each of the support services pages.

- Create links to other pages on the institution's Web site, such as to the faculty-staff-student directory.

- Create links to external sites that can serve as useful resources to students.

- Use a consistent format for the pages for the various support services.

- Consider the vocabulary of the Web page. Use terms easily understood by prospective and new students.

- Construct Web pages to be accessible to users with disabilities.

- Provide self-service options as much as possible, and make the procedures for using them easy to understand.

- Put forms on the Web page in downloadable format. If possible, enable students to complete and submit them online.

- On the Web page for each support service, provide the name and photo of a person who can answer additional questions. Provide phone and fax numbers and an e-mail address for reaching that person.

Support Services Prior to Enrollment

Information for Prospective and New Students

Institutions can use Web sites to provide a great deal of useful information to prospective distance students, regardless of the medium selected for the instruction. For ITV-based programs, Web sites can supplement and enhance informational meetings with prospective students at the community sites. For Web-based instruction, the fit is even better; retrieval of information about the institution's educational programs parallels the instructional medium itself.

For either situation, it is important to place a link for distance learning prominently on the home page of the institution. This link can then lead to a Web page offering a menu of information about the variety of programs and services for distance learners. It should also inform prospective students as clearly as possible about what is expected of them and what they can expect from the institution, the instructor, and various support services.

Elements to include on this Web site are the following:

a. Links to descriptions of various programs, certificates, and degrees offered through distance learning

b. Links to specific course descriptions (Some institutions provide study guides for many courses and also post these on the Web along with course syllabi.)

c. Information on costs

d. Information on the transferability of credits

e. Descriptions of admissions, registration, and advising requirements and procedures

f. Links to admissions staff

g. Thumbnail descriptions (and photos) of instructors, advisers, and key support staff

h. Descriptions of hardware and software requirements (For a good example cited in Krauth and Carbajal's [2000] *Guide to Developing Online Student Services,* see National University's Web site.[3])

    i.   Procedures for setting up a student Internet account at the institution

    j.   Photos of an ITV classroom or a streaming video excerpt from an ITV course

    k. Samples of a Web-based learning module

    l.   Links to pages outlining each of the support services noted earlier

    m. A list of frequently asked questions (FAQs) and responses to them, as exemplified by Cuesta College's FAQs[4]

It is important to provide phone numbers, fax numbers, and e-mail contacts for the person or team designated to assist distance learners, so that students can receive individual attention to their questions.

Some institutions also build into their Web sites a list of questions for prospective students designed to help them self-assess their preparedness and suitability for distance learning. Typical items in such an assessment tool ask students about their knowledge of the Internet, e-mail, word processing, and Web operations and their readiness to learn new communication skills; about their learning styles and preferences; and about the time they have available and their abilities to manage time. An example of a short self-assessment tool is the one developed by Linn-Benton Community College.[5] It can be submitted online and is then automatically scored and instantly returned to the sender along with informative feedback on each response chosen by the sender. Edmonds Community College has developed a self-assessment instrument (cited in the *Guide to Developing Online Student Services*, Krauth & Carbajal, 2000) that includes a number of questions about the prospective student's technical skills.[6] Prospective students should also be encouraged to discuss the questions on the self-assessment with admissions staff and advisers.

Admissions

Virtually all information relating to admissions can be put on a Web page, including admission application forms. Some institutions expect prospective students to print the forms, complete them in the traditional way, and submit them by mail, along with references and other supporting materials. Increasingly, institutions are enabling students to submit admission applications online, perhaps supplemented with mailed materials. Some permit the entire process to be done online. However the application process is accomplished, clear instructions should be given to the students, including information about admission prerequisites, procedures, and deadlines. If online application is feasible, consider incorporating an option allowing students to save and return to a partially completed application in case they don't have all the information needed at the time they begin working on the forms.

Differing requirements for various academic programs need to be clearly spelled out, as do rules concerning transfer of credit. Distance students are sometimes quite eclectic in selecting courses from a variety of higher education institutions. If they intend their studies to result in a degree, they must understand the transfer rules and residency requirements before enrolling. Some institutions have standing agreements with other higher education institutions concerning specific courses that will be accepted, and putting this information on the Web site is helpful.

We recommend providing students with an electronic or mailed confirmation that the admissions application has been received. Applicants should also be advised of an approximate date by which they can expect to learn whether they have been accepted for admission.

Several options should be available to students for paying admission application fees. Although an institution may have established a highly secure electronic payment system, many students are still not comfortable paying fees electronically with a credit card, and some do not have credit cards. Remittance by mailed checks or money orders should be permitted and a system devised that will reliably and speedily match payments to the application forms.

Financial Aid

Many students need financial assistance for enrollment in distance learning programs. The availability of financial aid is often the determining factor in students' decisions to pursue higher education and in their choice of an institution. It also affects the pace at which they complete their studies. Thus, making information about financial aid accessible to distance students is essential. Web pages can make detailed information instantly accessible as well as make it easy for students to apply for financial aid. The following information (at a minimum) should be included on the financial aid Web page:

a. Realistic estimates of the costs of distance education at the institution, including the costs of information access

b. Information about the institution's general policies and categories of financial aid (loans, scholarships, etc.) and the eligibility criteria for each

c. Information about the application process for financial aid

d. Information on how to reach the institution's financial aid counselors (names and photos, e-mail addresses, hours available) and a toll-free number to call

e. Timelines and deadlines for the financial aid process

f. A link to the institution's financial aid forms, so that they can be downloaded or completed online, for example, as at the University of New Mexico Web site[7]

g. Information about federal financial aid such as the Free Application for Federal Student Aid (FAFSA) and a link to the online FAFSA[8]

h. Links to other external resources for financial aid[9]

Academic Advising

Good advising is key to student retention and to students' progress toward completion of courses and programs. Much information helpful to students' planning can be put on institution Web pages, and the information can be organized in a way that maximizes the students' ability to make good choices. Institutions should facilitate personal contact between a distance student and a faculty or professional adviser. This contact is perhaps even more important than it is for a resident student. Distance students, like resident students, want to feel connected with the institution, but they lack the opportunities for the everyday, face-to-face contact with instructors, advisers, and peers that exist for on-campus students. In short, distance programs have to work harder than traditional on-campus programs to create a milieu supportive to students, and advisers have a key role to play in this process.

We will have more to say in Chapter 8 about the adviser's role and about ways to help create a community of learners whereby students can also be of assistance to each other. In the context of the present chapter, we suggest some ways that institutions can organize advising services for distance students:

a. Identify a specific person (faculty member or professional adviser) who will be available to the student throughout the period of his or her enrollment. Institutions differ in how they assign the advising function, depending on their resources, their traditions, and their staff. But however advising is assigned, the student deserves to be informed at the time of admission who the adviser will be and how to contact him or her.

b. Post information on faculty or staff advisers on the Web, including phone numbers, e-mail addresses, and a photo.

c. Install a toll-free phone number for students to connect with advisers.

d. Post on the Web the hours that advisers will be available to answer students' questions by phone or e-mail.

e. Post on the Web information on courses, majors, and degree requirements, so that it is readily accessible to students, advisers, and faculty.

f. Clarify whether the institution requires a student to secure the adviser's approval to register. If it does, enable advisers to give their approval online.

g. Post student handbooks and bulletin information on the Web.

h. Post on the Web downloadable forms needed to petition for course substitutions or waivers, to declare a major, to apply for graduation, and so on. If possible, enable students to submit these online.

i. Develop a system that affords students secure online access to their record of courses and grades. Various types of software for this are available commercially; some programs also let students update parts of their personal records, such as addresses and phone numbers.

Registration

Course registration can be accomplished online quickly and easily for both distance and resident students, and institutions have generally found it worthwhile to make the front-end investment required to accomplish this. Institutions using online access typically have cut the time required of students for registration from several hours (most of it spent standing in line) to just a few minutes. It is of even greater benefit to distance students, for whom a trip to campus may not be feasible. We recommend incorporating the following elements into Web pages for registration:

a. A description of the different ways that students can register: in person, online, or by mail, and the steps for doing each

b. Downloadable registration forms or instructions for online registration

c. Information on registration periods and priorities—who is permitted to register at what time

d. Course numbers, descriptions, and prerequisites

e. The schedule of classes, including instructional modality, instructors, meeting times (if synchronous instruction), and (for ITV) the locations of the various receiving sites

f. Information on course enrollment limits and, if possible, instantly updated information on the availability of each course (possible with some online registration software)

g. Links to segments of policy documents related to registration, such as institutional bulletins and handbooks

h. Links to faculty advisers' phone numbers and e-mail addresses

i. Information on late fees, course withdrawals and refunds, course cancellation policies, holds on registrations, and time limits for adding or canceling a course

j. A means for online confirmation of a student's registration in the courses selected

For an example of online registration incorporating these elements, visit the site developed by the University of Minnesota that is part of a more comprehensive student services package.[10]

Support Services for Enrolled Students

Bookstore Services

Campus bookstores can serve distance students through the Internet as fully as they serve resident students. Consider these aspects in setting up bookstore services for distance learners:

a. Enable students to shop online for textbooks, course packets, supplies, and other items.

b. Enable students to quickly access information on the required and supplementary texts for each course, prices, and whether new and used copies are available.

c. Permit students to submit an online request to reserve copies of texts that have not yet arrived at the bookstore.

d. Display images of some of the nonbook merchandise, including clothing and other articles carrying the institution's name—items that can help students identify with the institution.

e. Set up the Web page on the shopping cart model, whereby a student can click on an item and add it to the order.

f. Provide for online confirmation of the order.

g. Enable students to pay by mail or online with a credit card.

h. Provide for U.S. mail or package delivery service to students' homes or offices.

i. If possible, design the system so students can check online to see whether the order has been shipped.

j. Post the bookstore's policies on merchandise returns and on textbook buy-back policies.

Library Services

Critics of distance education sometimes cite the difficulty of providing library services as its biggest drawback. Yet as technology has improved, library services have become similar for distance and resident students. More and more information is becoming available online, including hundreds of searchable online journal indexes, full texts of many journals and books, electronic databases, and splendid archives of images and documents for use in courses in almost every field. Resident students do still have an advantage of being able to wander through the campus library's stacks to locate related materials and to quickly check out printed material. Campus libraries, however, are rapidly developing ways to extend services to distance students, including the following suggestions:

a. Set up an electronic reserve system that puts assigned course readings online (with permission from the copyright holders); students can quickly access these items without having to purchase a course packet.

b. Post on the Web information about the full range of library resources and services and create a library Web page specifically for distance learners (see, for example, the University of Minnesota Libraries' Web page for distance learning[11]).

c. Assign certain library staff members to focus on working with distance learners, and post that information on the library's distance learning Web pages.

d. Provide distance students online access to electronic resources (indexes, full text materials, etc.), and provide easy-to-understand instructions for accessing material.

e. Provide reference services through a toll-free number and through e-mail.

f. Work with ITV course instructors and community or campus libraries near the distant sites to make materials available locally.

g. Make it possible for students to borrow books and materials by U.S. or private mail and send some documents (for example, those in the public domain or others with no copyright restrictions) electronically or by fax.

h. Establish the means for students to request materials online.

i. Post information on interlibrary loan policies and procedures.

j. Create links on the Web pages to resources providing guidance on how to develop term papers and other projects, how to search for information, how to evaluate information, and how to cite sources.

Readers will find the *Guidelines for Distance Learning Library Services* published by the Association of College and Research Libraries helpful in their own distance education programs.[12]

Technical Support

Distance education demands adequate technical support. For ITV-based programs, this means equipping electronic classrooms and training technical support staff to operate the equipment and to fix problems that may arise during the transmission of classes. ITV students themselves need only a few instructions concerning use of microphones (and a few other instructions concerning electronic classroom etiquette) to become fully engaged. For Web-based courses and for Web-enhanced ITV courses, however, students will need considerably more technical help, both before and during the course. Course instructors can give limited assistance with some problems, but typically they do not want to spend much time on technical support, viewing it as a distraction from their main tasks of teaching the course content. Moreover, many instructors do not have sufficient expertise to be of real help to students. It is better to set up a "Help Desk" staffed by persons who understand the hardware and software. Many institutions already have a Help Desk in place for resident students, faculty, and staff, and service to distance learners can be added to it. Assistance should be available for extended hours because many online students do their coursework in the late evening or early morning, and some programs may serve students in different time zones. The following points should be kept in mind when setting up technical support:

a. Develop a training module for each instructional template used by the institution, which students can use to learn their way around Web-enhanced or Web-based courses. For an example, visit the WebCT training module used at the University of Minnesota.[13]

b. Encourage prospective and new students to consult with the Help Desk before selecting computer hardware and software for purchase, or create Web pages and handouts clearly explaining which hardware and software is appropriate for the program.

c. Set up a Web page describing the technical support services available, their hours, and who is eligible to use them.

d. Provide a toll-free number for students seeking technical support, and advertise it on the program or course Web pages.

e. Create a listserv for students enrolled in the distance education programs so they can be notified in advance of changes in hours or interruptions in technical support.

f. Develop and post on the Web a detailed set of frequently asked questions (FAQs) for troubleshooting problems with hardware and software.

Tutoring

Tutoring occurs in several contexts in distance education. In some institutions, independent study coupled with individualized instruction is the central activity of a course. In others, tutoring is an optional, supplementary form of support intended for those students needing extra help. The tutor may be the instructor, a teaching assistant, or another staff member assigned specifically to this task. Some institutions provide special staff for tutoring in certain areas, such as writing skills.

Tutoring at a distance can be accomplished by e-mail, telephone, fax, or regular mail, as in traditional correspondence courses. The Internet also opens up possibilities for group tutoring and for peer tutoring through use of chat rooms or online discussion groups. In Chapter 8, we will discuss how peer-to-peer arrangements can build a learning community that also helps sustain students' motivation and retention.

Consider the following suggestions when setting up tutoring services:

a. Afford students tutoring online or by phone if possible, so that feedback is more immediate.

b. Post on the Web information about the availability of tutoring or other instructional support, noting times and phone numbers of staff.

c. Provide a toll-free number if tutoring is made available by telephone.

d. Post on the Web suggestions on how to study, how to take tests, how to use group sessions on the Internet, and so on (also see Chapter 3).

e. Create links to external resources on effective studying.

Services for Distance Learners With Disabilities

There are three main reasons for organizing an institution's distance education program so that it is accessible to distance learners with disabilities. First, institutions have a legal obligation to do so. Second, an ethical obligation arises because distance education may be the best (and in some situations the only) available means to an education for some individuals with disabilities. Third, today's society needs competent, reliable workers. We cannot afford to overlook any person's potential (Paist, 1995).

Section 504 of the Rehabilitation Act of 1973 and the Americans With Disabilities Act of 1990 make unlawful the exclusion from educational programs of otherwise qualified individuals with disabilities, as a matter of civil rights. Institutions, faculty, and staff must make services accessible by making *reasonable accommodation*. In doing so, however, institutions have a legal right to "provide the accommodation that guarantees students equal access to services at the most reasonable cost to the institution and to request documentation of disability once a student has enrolled" (Paist, 1995, p. 62). In seeking to comply with the law, some institutions have developed guidelines to help campuses, departments, and faculty members create accommodation for distance learners (Carnevale, 1999). For example, the California Community Colleges System (1999) has published a comprehensive set of guidelines for online accessibility.

Beyond the legalities, however, is a growing realization that the flexibility in time, space, and media encompassed by distance learning can have special advantages compared with traditional classroom education in creating access for students with disabilities. Students with mobility impairment benefit from having courses delivered to their homes or offices. Students who are hearing impaired may learn better from Web-based courses than from traditional lectures. Students with certain types of learning disabilities may benefit from being able to control the pace of learning, rather than having to try to keep up with classmates. As experience with distance courses becomes more widespread, the number of distance learners who have disabilities may be expected to grow.

The term *disability* encompasses a broad range of individual situations. Experience suggests that the most satisfactory outcomes for students with disabilities occur when individuals' needs are considered case by case, with reference to the student's particular situation and the course or courses planned. Most institutions have a designated office or staff person to assist students with disabilities. To be effective, this office must be involved early in the planning with both student and instructor(s). Paist (1995) notes that "information, consultation, and expert advice can be obtained from many outside sources to supplement that provided by the student" (p. 64), such as vocational rehabilitation agencies, health care providers, other assessment professionals, campus disability offices, advocacy groups, and so on. Paist identifies and describes in considerable detail the various aspects of providing services to students with disabilities enrolled with University of Wisconsin Extension Independent Study.

Inform students with disabilities or their advocates about the services provided. All course catalogs, student handbooks, course guides, and registration materials should include an explanation of the institution's policy concerning the rights and responsibilities of students with disabilities. For example, all independent study course guides at the University of Wisconsin include the following statement:

> Independent Study is committed to providing reasonable accommodation for students with disabilities. Such accommodation includes making course materials available in accessible delivery formats (for example, large print, cassette tape, scripts, and computer disk) and adapting written assignment and exam procedures as appropriate. If you are a student with disabilities and would like to discuss accommodation, please contact Independent Study (608-263-2055; toll-free: 800-442-6460; TTY: 608-262-8662). We ask that you request alternate, accessible course delivery formats at least eight weeks before beginning work on the course, and testing and written-assignment accommodation well in advance of need. (Paist, 1995, p. 65)

The disabilities services office also sends a letter to vocational rehabilitation field offices inviting counselors to consider the program's suitability for their clients and to refer them to the office.

Plan for each student's accommodation needs on a case-by-case basis. Each individual's needs are different, and students then are more likely to feel their needs are understood. Many institutions find it useful to appoint a disabilities liaison who communicates both with students and with faculty and support services staff, sometimes serving as an advocate. Assigning the liaison tasks to the same staff member(s) helps the institution accumulate knowledge about disabilities and use that information in its planning.

Students with disabilities need accessible instruction. This may mean communication via a different medium. Students who are visually impaired may need to submit their assignments on tape rather than in writing, and instructors may need to tape-record, rather than write, their comments on the work. Some students who are learning disabled may need more time to complete assignments. E-mail or a teletypewriter (TTY) connection may work best for some students who are hearing impaired (Paist, 1995).

Course materials need to be made accessible. Large-size print, Braille, scripts, or captioning may be the best choice in some situations. Getting print materials into an electronic format enables the content to be converted electronically to other formats, such as Braille or synthesized speech. Many works used in college courses are also available through sources such as Project Gutenberg,[14] the Oxford Text Archive,[15] and Recording for the Blind & Dyslexic[16] (Paist, 1995). For students who are hearing impaired, scripts of audiotapes and captioning of video materials can be provided. Paist notes that "it is best—and cheapest—to plan ahead and make the scripts or captions as the tape is being developed" (p. 68), rather than later, when the process is more expensive and time-consuming. Likewise, it is much less expensive to design Web pages at the outset with accommodation of disabilities in mind; it is much more expensive to redesign them later (Carnevale, 1999).

Make the means for testing accessible. Paist (1995) comments that the accommodations may include arranging for students to take a proctored exam at their own sites or involve changing the test format (although not the content), for example, allowing an oral instead of a written exam, permitting students to tape their answers, changing from a fill-in-the-blank test to a multiple-choice format, allowing more time to complete the exam, reducing or eliminating distractions, and so on. The Association for Higher Education and Disability is a source of excellent publications on testing accommodations.[17] Students with disabilities are expected to demonstrate as much knowledge of the course content as other students; the means for assessing the knowledge, however, may need to be altered.

Offer support and training to faculty and staff on accommodating disabilities. Instructors need to know well ahead of time about the needs of students who will be enrolled in their classes, as do advisers and other support services staff. The liaison staff alerts the appropriate people as soon as a student with a verified disability has contacted their office, emphasizing that program staff will help solve accommodation needs and also that instructors have a legal and moral obligation to provide reasonable accommodations. Occasional workshops for faculty and staff on typical disabilities and accommodations are also helpful in raising awareness and in providing information.

Federal and state sources of funding are available for accommodation and for research on accommodation. It will be useful in locating this funding to talk with the same agencies that provide help with assessment and accommodation, such as a state division of vocational rehabilitation (Paist, 1995).

As with other support services, the Web is an important tool for serving distance students with disabilities. The *Guide to Developing On-line Student Services* (Krauth & Carbajal, 2000) referred to previously includes the following suggestions for all Web pages used by distance learners:

a. Create a text-only version of all Web pages.

b. Use the *Web Content Accessibility Guidelines* (W3C), which explain how to make Web content more accessible to persons with disabilities.[18]

c. Test Web pages using *Bobby,* a free service provided by the Center for Applied Special Technology to "help Web page authors identify and repair significant barriers to access by individuals with disabilities."[19]

d. Include on the Web page general information about services for students with disabilities and laws and policies regarding access and accommodation. Identify the disabilities that qualify, and make clear what documentation is required to receive services.

e.   Describe the types of services available.

f.   Create links to other useful sites with information for students with disabilities, rather than duplicating effort. The links page developed by Illinois State University is suggested as an exemplar by Krauth and Carbajal's *Guide*.[20] Also helpful are the WebAble site[21] and the University of Toronto Special Needs Opportunity Windows (SNOW) site.[22] The latter has a particularly useful page concerning adaptive technology, such as alternative keyboards, alternative mouse systems, optical character recognition, personal data assistants, refreshable Braille displays, screen magnifiers, screen readers, text-to-speech systems, and voice recognition systems.

g.   Post a faculty and staff guide for working with students with disabilities.

h.   Consider developing a Web page concerning career information specifically for students with disabilities.

In sum, distance education can be made accessible to distance students with disabilities. With advance planning and coordination of instructors, students, the office of disabilities services, and other support staff, accommodation can be accomplished.

Support Services After Course or Program Completion

An institution should continue its relationship with distance students after they have completed their programs of study for several important reasons. First, many of the students will need some continuing services, such as transcripts and career services. Second, reinforcing distance students' identification with the institution is mutually beneficial: The students gain from pride in affiliation, and the institution gains loyal supporters. Third, distance students who have previously taken courses or degrees from the institution may later decide to take additional courses or degrees from the institution and may refer others as prospective students. Thus, alumni of distance courses are also important for the continuing marketing of the program. For all these reasons, it is important to stay in touch with those who have completed courses or degrees. Suggestions for ways to reinforce the connection are described below.

Staying in Touch

a. Make it easy for alumni to update their addresses and other personal information, preferably online.

b. Enable alumni to easily request and receive transcripts, including downloadable prints of their unofficial transcripts.

c. Encourage alumni to join alumni associations and other alumni activities, and post updates of activities on the Web.

d. Encourage alumni to subscribe to a listserv from the institution. Use the listserv, along with the Web and regular mail, to inform alumni and others about credit and noncredit continuing education offerings.

Career Services

Career services are an important resource for students, both while enrolled and after graduation. Typical services include working with students and alumni to help them identify their career focus; helping students and alumni develop a strong résumé; helping students sharpen interviewing skills; providing information and resources about careers, employers, and specific job vacancies; providing workshops relating to career opportunities; maintaining a placement service and system for sending résumés to prospective employers; communicating principles for negotiating and evaluating job offers; organizing job fairs, company information sessions, and on-site company interviews; and facilitating networking with employers and alumni. Not all these services can be provided at a distance. For example, mock interviewing (simulation of the interview situation, coupled with feedback to the student or alumnus) should simulate as realistically as possible the typical situation, which in many cases means face-to-face interviewing. Videoconferencing and telephone interviewing are sometimes also used to interview applicants, however, and these modalities can be offered to distance students and alumni. Likewise, job fairs and company information sessions are conducted on campus. But many other career services can be offered at a distance through the Web, by e-mail, or with CD-ROMs or videotapes.

The Web can be useful for communicating career services information to distance learners in several ways:

a. List the full array of career services offered by the institution and who is eligible to use them. Potential users include alumni, current students, prospective students, employers, and others in the community.

b. Include descriptions of opportunities to gain valuable experience such as internships, part-time employment, volunteer activities, and international work-study possibilities.

c. Create links to online tools that can help learners assess their values, preferences, interests, and skills.

d. Post information describing career paths that can result from the various majors offered.

e. Create a link to the *U.S. Occupational Outlook Handbook* and other career resource handbooks.[23]

f. Post basic information about preparing a résumé, professional etiquette, tips for interviewing, how to follow up an interview, and so on.

g. Post information on current job openings, local and nationwide. Some institutions require a password for access to these listings; others make them available to anyone.

h. Create listservs for current job openings organized by major to which students and alumni can subscribe.

i. Create job search links that will help alumni and students connect to interactive job search Web sites, job listing Web sites, and sites specific to jobs open in particular degrees or majors.

j. Create links to professional associations and job registries associated with the various majors offered by the institution.

k. Consider developing a searchable online database of alumni and others who are willing to share career experiences and tips by e-mail with current students and alumni.

l. Enable alumni and students to register online for placement services, submit materials online, and receive employer contact information online. Some institutions have also developed an automated system whereby employers are automatically sent résumés of prospective applicants who fit their criteria. For an example of an automated recruiting system, see the CARS system at the University of Minnesota

Carlson School of Management.[24] Also worthy of note is a project sponsored by the Learning Anytime Anywhere Partnership and funded by the U.S. Department of Education's Fund for the Improvement of Postsecondary Education—"Beyond the Administrative Core: Creating Web-Based Student Services for Online Learners." It is expected to result in

> a commercially developed package of web-based services, including those not currently available from any software company; student services modules developed at four partner institutions; a set of guidelines for institutions interested in building their own "home-grown" web-based services; and detailed accounts of the institutional change processes required to implement an array of web-based services.[25]

Summary

In this chapter, we have discussed various ways that institutions can support learners at a distance. Students will be more encouraged to enroll in distance education if support services are delivered in user-friendly ways that reduce or minimize traveling to campus. The Web can be used to deliver a wide array of support services, and resident students also benefit from this mode of access. We listed some principles for Web design that apply to most or all the support services, such as the following:

- Creating a link on the institution's home page to a page exclusively for distance learning programs

- Linking the distance education Web pages to the pages for various support services

- Creating links to advisers, financial aid counselors, admissions and registration staff, and others, and providing cost-free ways to contact them

- Using a consistent format for Web pages

- Making forms downloadable or returnable online

- Providing FAQs and self-assessment tools

- Making instruction, support services, and Web pages accessible to persons with disabilities

- Creating links to external resources

We also encourage institutions to develop or adapt software packages—several are now available commercially—that offer a comprehensive array of support services online. Underlying all these suggestions is the view that distance students are an important and growing constituency for higher education institutions. The development of new technologies makes it possible to serve these students, who differ from traditional college students in many ways. Institutions that view distance learners as valuable resources and that carefully design support services to serve them will reap dividends in the form of satisfied and loyal learners and an enhanced reputation for delivering a quality program.

WWw ▸   At our Sage Web site, www.sagepub.com/mehrotra

On our companion Web site are links to institutions providing exemplary support services to distance learners. There are lists of additional resources for students with disabilities and institutions seeking to make their distance courses more accessible.

Notes

1. www.wiche.edu/telecom/resources/publications/index.htm
2. www.outreach.washington.edu/dl/
3. www.online.nu.edu/index.real?action=technical
4. http://library.cuesta.cc.ca.us/distance/faqs.htm
5. http://cf.lbcc.cc.or.us/disted/de_survey.cfm
6. http://online.edcc.edu/selfassess.html
7. www.unm.edu/~finaid/eform01/
8. www.fafsa.ed.gov/
9. www.finaid.org and www.collegenet.com

10. www.onestop.umn.edu/enrollment/enroll.html
11. www.lib.umn.edu/dist/
12. www.ala.org/acrl/
13. www3.extension.umn.edu/media/module0/
14. www.gutenberg.net/
15. www.ota.ahds.ac.uk/ota/index.html
16. www.rfbd.org/
17. www.ahead.org
18. www.w3.org/TR/WCAG/
19. www.cast.org/bobby/
20. www.ilstu.edu/depts/disabilityconcerns/links.shtml
21. www.Webable.com/aboutsite.html
22. snow.utoronto.ca/learn_tech.html
23. http://stats.bls.gov/ocohome.htm
24. www.csom.umn.edu/
25. www.wiche.edu/telecom/projects/laap/index.htm

References

Americans With Disabilities Act, 42 U.S.C.A., § 12101 *et seq.* (West 1993).

California Community Colleges. (1999). *Distance education: Access guidelines for students with disabilities.* Sacramento, CA: Office of the Chancellor.

Carnevale, D. (1999). Colleges strive to give disabled students access to on-line courses. *Chronicle of Higher Education, 46*(10), A69-A70.

Dirr, P. J. (1999, December). *Putting principles into practice: Promoting effective support services for students in distance learning programs: A report on the findings of a survey* [Online]. Retrieved from the World Wide Web: www.wiche.edu/telecom/resources/publications/index.htm (Available from the Western Cooperative for Educational Telecommunications, P.O. Box 9752, Boulder, CO 80301)

Krauth, B., & Carbajal, J. (2000). *Guide to developing online student services.* Boulder, CO: Western Cooperative for Educational Telecommunications.

Paist, E. H. (1995). Serving students with disabilities in distance education programs. *American Journal of Distance Education, 9*(1), 61-70.

Phipps, R. A., Wellman, J. V., & Merisotis, J. P. (1998). *Assuring quality in distance learning: A preliminary review.* Washington, DC: Council for Higher Education Accreditation.

Rehabilitation Act of 1973, Pub. L. No. 93-112, § 504, 29 U.S.C. § 794.

8

Ensuring High Completion Rates

The enrollment of a student—whether distance or traditional—in a program represents an investment of resources by the institution and by the student. This is true even before the student participates in the first session of the first course. The institution has already invested resources in recruiting, admitting, and advising that student. Likewise, the student has invested time and money in finding the program, securing necessary equipment and study materials, and paying tuition. Both parties, therefore, have an interest in the completion of the planned program of study. Students who drop out represent at least some wasted resources. Moreover, one important criterion used by students, parents, college guidebooks, accrediting bodies, legislatures, and others to evaluate and compare higher education institutions is the percentage of students who complete the program (Shale & Gomes, 1998). Some state legislatures have begun to link appropriations to completion rates (Reisberg, 1999). Institutions thus have good reasons to be concerned about their completion rates. In this chapter, we discuss the problem of noncompletion or dropout in general and with reference to distance programs. We then suggest some strategies for reducing the problem in distance education programs.

The Problem of Retention

Although drop-out rates at some institutions have remained steady during the last decade, those of other institutions have increased somewhat. Not surprisingly, a 1998 study conducted by the American College Testing Program found that drop-out rates are lowest (8.8%) at the most selective institutions and highest (46.2%) at the least selective institutions (cited in Reisberg, 1999). Some observers attribute declining completion rates to the strong U.S. economy, whose immediate rewards appeal to many students more than attending college does. In the case of community colleges, the decline probably also reflects the reality that for-profit institutions and online courses are cutting into the market of adult, part-time learners who historically have been served by these institutions. Some community colleges have hired consultants to help them with the issue of student retention (Lords, 2000). Other institutions with lower completion rates have initiated special efforts to retain students, such as creating a small residential college-within-a-college for freshmen and promoting learning communities in which small groups of students meet regularly to study and bond with each other (Reisberg, 1999). The main focus of many of these programs is to encourage greater social interaction of students on campus to produce a greater sense of belonging, increased retention, and improved educational outcomes (Wisely & Jorgensen, 2000).

Retention in Distance Education Programs

The completion rates of distance programs also deserve scrutiny. Although no national data on completion rates yet exist for distance programs, data have been collected at some institutions. According to Carr (2000), these studies have generally suggested that distance programs do tend to have somewhat lower course completion and program retention rates than do comparable residential programs. Carr observes,

Although there is significant variation among institutions—with some reporting course-completion rates of more than 80 percent and others finding that fewer than 50 percent of distance-education students finish their courses—several administrators concur that course-completion rates are often 10 to 20 percentage points higher in traditional courses than in distance offerings. (p. A39)

Factors Affecting Completion Rates in Distance Education Programs

Various explanations have been suggested for lower completion rates of distance students than those of residential students. Some explanations focus on student characteristics, some on instructor characteristics, some on institutional supports (or the lack thereof), and some on the nature of distance learning itself.

Student Characteristics. Student characteristics suggested as contributing to higher drop-out rates among distance students include having heavier time commitments to work and family responsibilities and more frequent changes of employment. Of course, it is precisely these demands that motivate many individuals to select distance courses instead of traditional courses because distance education affords greater flexibility in schedule and reduces or eliminates commuting time. Some experts even argue that distance students in their late teens and early 20s are more at risk of noncompletion because older students may be better able to work independently (Carr, 2000).

Other studies have focused on the preparedness of students for distance learning, such as work habits, capacity for self-direction, self-confidence, and so on. For example, Carr, Fullerton, Severino, and McHugh (1996) found in a study of a 2-year distance program in nurse-midwifery that the best predictors of completion were related to the students' approaches to studying. Students who dropped out were "less aggressive in their study habits, less likely to use the resources of a study partner, less likely to allocate sufficient time for their studies, and less likely to use the modes of communication that were available" (p. 127). Carr et al. note that their findings are similar to those from other studies, in that demographic characteristics were "less predictive of continuation in an educational program than was the degree of social support received during the program of studies" (p. 127). Similarly, Greer, Hudson, and Paugh (1998) found in a study of adult online learners that the most common themes in students' perceptions of success were budgeting time, being self-motivated, and having supportive friends and family. Parker (1995) found students' lack of time management skills and ill-defined educational goals to be the primary reasons noncompleters gave for dropping out. Fjortoft (1996) found in a study of a distance program in pharmacy that the level of students' comfort with individualized learning was a significant factor in predicting continuance in the program. Students' learning styles also have been found to be related to the drop-out rate (Terrell & Dringus, 1999-2000).

Instructor Characteristics. Instructor inexperience with distance education and poor teaching may be important factors in student drop-out. Some students who drop out complain that they have not received personal attention and that there is a lack of immediate feedback from instructors (Carr, 2000). Some authorities argue that this aspect of the drop-out problem will diminish through time, however, because distance technology is continually improving and because faculty members are rapidly gaining experience as more and more institutions offer distance programs and courses. Evidence for the growth of distance education is found in a survey commissioned by the National Education Association (NEA, 2000). It reveals that currently 1 in 10 higher education NEA members teaches a distance course and that 90% of NEA members teaching traditional courses report that distance learning courses are offered or being considered at their institution. It seems likely that a high proportion of faculty across a wide array of institutions will soon have experience with distance instruction.

Support Services. Some institutions that have developed distance courses and degree programs continue to deliver student support services only in the traditional way. As we discussed in Chapter 7, it is often difficult for distance learners to come to campus for advising, orientation, tutoring, and meetings with the instructor. Luedtke (1999) found that although distance education programs in Texas public 2-year community and technical colleges provided a great deal of information on the Web, students in many of the programs still had to go to the campus for advising and counseling services. Also, learning resources, such as libraries and electronic databases, were accessible through only 77% of the Web sites. If distance students' access to needed services is limited, it should not surprise us that more of them become discouraged or feel isolated and drop out.

The Nature of Distance Education. Some educators maintain that we should *expect* distance completion rates to be lower than those for residential programs, given that distance students typically do not engage in full-time study and that earning a degree entirely through part-time study becomes a lengthy and daunting undertaking. Instead, it is quite typical for a student to take only one or several courses by distance education, sometimes because they fill a particular gap in a person's education, because they are courses specified by an employer, or because students shop around for distance courses that can be applied to degree programs at other institutions (Shale & Gomes, 1998). Other writers maintain that distance education inevitably entails a reduction in student-faculty and student-student interaction and that because the amount of person-to-person interaction is central to retention, distance course and program drop-out rates will always be higher than rates for residential students. In rebuttal, some educators hold that the interaction between faculty and students and among students is sometimes greater in distance education than in traditional courses and that the level of interaction depends on how the courses are structured. No doubt there is considerable variation in the level of interaction among programs and among courses within the same program. Moreover, students' expectations concerning the interaction required of them also vary considerably. Those who expect intensive interaction but find the interaction level quite low are probably more inclined to drop out than those whose experience matches their expectations.

Our view on completion rates is that many factors contribute to student completion and that each of the factors previously cited probably contributes partially to dropout by distance students. We agree that person-to-person interaction is central to the problem, but we think that distance programs can do a number of things to increase course and program completion rates. In the remainder of this chapter, we suggest some strategies for improving retention.

Strategies for Improving Completion Rates

In this section, we recommend several active measures that a distance education program can implement to address the problem of low completion rates.

Realize that higher education is in a new environment. Distance learners' motivations, needs, and plans are typically much more varied than those of resident students. The working assumptions and stereotypes held by faculty, staff, and administrators about student characteristics need to be thoroughly reexamined—educators are dealing now with new constituencies, or, in business terms, with new markets. Therefore, it is important to conduct a thorough assessment of students' needs, perceptions, and preferences prior to launching a distance education program (Chapter 2). A study of the program preferences of potential students in relation to course type, delivery method, and time availability found that there was no "average" student and that no one program could satisfy the needs of all students. Instead, four segments of the student population were identified, each with distinct preferences. After considering this information, the program (an engineering education consortium) then could focus on one or more segments based on students' program preferences and the resources needed to provide the program (Bunn & Barnes, 1999). With the spread of distance education, and especially of online learning, many students now have a much wider choice of educational opportunities than they did previously. Most institutions cannot afford to assume that they will continue to receive and retain students from their traditional constituencies in the same numbers as before.

Do thorough preadmission counseling. This will help both the students and the institution determine if the distance program is a good fit with the students' interests, abilities, and preparation. Some students may not sufficiently realize the extent of the demands that distance learning will make on them in working independently, in doing homework, in staying on schedule, in locating resources, in interacting with other students electronically, and in participating fully in the course in general. As a result, they may become discouraged and drop out. Thus, institutions need to educate prospective students about the "facts of life" concerning distance learning as early as possible and to help those who are unprepared—either by assisting them in gaining the requisite skills for success in a distance education program or by encouraging them not to enroll. Written materials can be used to supplement one-on-one counseling. Zajkowski (1993) found that a preenrollment counseling booklet made a difference in the completion rates for prospective business students in New Zealand. Although institutional resources must be committed to preadmission counseling, the investment will benefit both the students and the institution.

Treat each student as an individual. This old admonition is especially relevant to distance education. A key variable in student retention is the extent to which students feel recognized and appreciated as individuals. This implies that faculty and staff who have direct contact with students must work harder than ever to become acquainted with students as individuals. In addition to initiating communication with individual students, some instructors take steps such as posting on the course Web site photographs that were taken on the first day of class (with students' permission). Other instructors facilitate student-created Web pages or encourage active use of a course bulletin board (Morley & LaMaster, 1999).

Respond as soon as possible to students' questions and comments. The rapidity of the instructor's response affects students' feelings of connection to the distance program. Many distance instructors set aside a specific time each day when they respond by phone or e-mail to students' questions. As we commented in Chapter 3, it is also helpful to provide toll-free phone numbers to make it easier for students to call.

Initiate communication with students. Be proactive. Phone calls and e-mails from staff, advisers, and instructors can make a big difference in the extent to which students feel connected with the institution. Distance learning requires instructors and staff to be the initiators of communication with students more than is true for residential instruction, in which students and instructors typically see each other two or three times a week or more. Distance education calls for something of a change from the traditional faculty-student relationship, in which faculty are usually in a reactive role in communicating individually with students. In a study of commuter students, Johnson (1997) found that faculty-student and staff-student interaction and connection were the most important characteristics distinguishing the retained students from those who dropped out.

Faculty and administrators considering distance education sometimes are concerned that it requires substantially more time for interaction with students outside class than does resident instruction. Indeed it does. The NEA study (2000) found an enormous amount of faculty-student communication, most of it by e-mail:

> Eighty-three percent (83%) of faculty teaching web-based courses use email to communicate with a typical student in their class once a week or more. Almost half (42%) of faculty teaching non-web-based courses use email to communicate with a typical student once a week or more. (p. 23)

Telephone contact was used by 85% of faculty at least once during the semester, with about half of the faculty using phone contact at least twice a month.

The NEA study (2000) also found that

> faculty teaching courses with more student interaction are more likely than their counterparts with less student interaction to hold an overall more positive [attitude] toward their distance course. Faculty with frequent student interaction also give their distance learning course higher ratings on meeting the goals NEA has determined are essential to a quality education. In terms of these benchmarks, distance learning courses with more interaction are more successful. (p. 24)

Thus, communicating with distance students individually is important for sustaining students' motivation as well as for communicating and clarifying instructional content. The evidence suggests that more frequent communication is more likely to increase the retention of distance learners.

Secure student feedback early and often. Both instructors and support staff of distance programs should secure feedback from students early in their studies. Some feedback can be obtained through one-on-one conversations (often by phone or e-mail), and some can be secured through brief feedback forms supplied online or at the end of an ITV class session. Collecting this information sends a message to the students that the instructor and institution are concerned about their learning, and it also provides the instructor or staff member with information useful both for assisting individual students and for making program adjustments. Early feedback is especially helpful. Chyung, Winiecki, and Fenner (1998) found that satisfaction during the first or second courses was the major factor that decided whether adult distance students continued with their program of studies.

Help students learn to use the technology. McElhinney and Nasseh (1998-1999) identify four challenges for students in online courses: (a) mastering computer-based pedagogy, (b) mastering the skills of learning from computers, (c) mastering the content they intend to learn, and (d) mastering the skills required to communicate evidence of their learning to faculty members. Although faculty new to distance instruction may tend to focus mainly on the third and fourth skills, learning must occur in all four areas for a student to do well in Web-based learning. Particularly with students new to online learning or to the Web itself, it is important for the instructor to spend time with students introducing the technology and giving examples of how it can best be used. Many institutions also provide a Web site tutorial to guide students step-by-step in how best to use the various options and features of instructional Web sites. (For an example of such a tutorial for WebCT, see the University of Minnesota Module Zero.[1]) As we suggested in Chapter 7, setting up a help line will assist students with troubles they encounter in accessing or using Web sites.

Extend counseling services to distance students. Most institutions provide residential students with counseling for personal difficulties interfering with their studies. Distance students also may need these services, and having counseling available may prevent these students from dropping out. A problem is how best to deliver counseling services because coming to a campus counseling office is sometimes just not feasible. Some institutions with distance programs provide no alternative to the campus office, but others are increasingly establishing telephone lines for this purpose. Although telephone counseling does not enable the full range of visual and auditory communication, it can still be of great help to many students. In a survey of institutions within the service area of the Western Interstate Commission for

Higher Education (WICHE), Dirr (1999) found that only 44% of the institutions offered personal counseling services to distance learners. Of those, most offered counseling through a toll-free telephone number. A few institutions with distance programs contract for counseling services with local community agencies, but this is still rare, probably both because of fiscal reasons and because students in many distance programs are dispersed across wide geographic areas. Dirr found that only 2% of the institutions provided online counseling services and only 5% had established cooperative agreements with community providers. Students, however, can also be encouraged to use sources of support and counseling in their home communities, and the institution can help in some cases by making a referral to local community resources.

Build community among the participants in a distance course. Building community means creating opportunities for students to interact with other students in the course, to exchange ideas, to learn from other students' views, and to identify with other students as fellow class members. Chat rooms and electronic bulletin boards can help to create community in distance courses by facilitating students' exchanges of ideas (McCollum, 1997). Courses that enable students to do so are likely to have fewer students dropping out than courses in which almost the only interactions are those between student and instructor. In the latter case, there are fewer ties holding the students' interest in the course and sustaining the students' motivation. Moreover, building community enhances students' learning. There is considerable evidence that combining participatory and collaborative instructional techniques with presentation of content results in as much or more learning than presentation of content only (Boling & Robinson, 1999; Johnson, Johnson, & Smith, 1991; Schwitzer & Lovell, 1999).

It is also good to have variety in the instructional format. Well-chosen exercises and assignments can thus help to both retain students' interest and motivation and increase the learning that occurs. An example of an online community-building exercise that accomplishes both is the "Murder on the Internet" exercise created by Terri Nelson and Walter Oliver at California State University at San Bernardino for intermediate college-level classes in French and Spanish.[2] The game requires students to solve a murder mystery. It is played in four rounds, each lasting approximately 2 weeks. Various resources are distributed on the

Internet, such as diary entries, wills, newspaper articles, police reports, and maps. The game teaches linguistic and critical thinking skills by requiring students to intensively communicate with each other via the Internet to solve the murder. Students' vocabularies and grammar skills are built by requiring them to communicate with each other only in the language under study and by requiring final projects that compile evidence and reach a conclusion. Evidently, students in these courses have been quite enthusiastic about the exercise and the amount they learned. They requested that the game be moved from a supplementary position to a main course activity. Course attendance also increased, and more students decided to do a major or minor in the language than had previously been the case.

Improvements in distance education technology are also facilitating community building. Utah State University, for example, uses a teleconferencing system that delivers both voice and video via the Internet. This technology allows face-to-face interaction among students and between students and university personnel in various learning and support situations, such as advising and mentoring students, conducting study group sessions, delivering didactic courses, supervising practical courses, and training local cooperating teachers (Menlove, Hansford, & Lignugaris-Kraft, 2000).

Summary Tips

Retention of students is a problem for both residential and distance education programs. For distance programs, we observed that student characteristics, instructor characteristics, support services, and the nature of distance education probably all contribute to some extent to student dropout. Although some attrition of distance learners is probably inevitable, programs can implement strategies to reduce student dropout so that more students complete their studies, including the following:

- Carefully assessing students' needs

- Investing resources in preenrollment counseling

- Treating each student as an individual

- Responding quickly to students' communications
- Initiating communication with students
- Securing early student feedback and using it for course and program improvement
- Extending personal counseling services to students
- Building community among students, faculty, and staff

In combination, these strategies should increase students' motivation to persist in their studies and thereby increase the rate of course and program completion.

WWw ▸ At our Sage Web site, www.sagepub.com/mehrotra

Our companion Web site has additional references on student retention and factors affecting completion rates. There are also links to exemplary Web pages helping students determine if distance education is a good fit to their needs and learning styles. Other links connect with tips and resources for maintaining effective communication with distance students and examples of innovative techniques for building community among distance learners.

Notes

1. www3.extension.umn.edu/media/module0/
2. http://flan.csusb.edu/dept/vu_info/mmclass.htm

References

Boling, N., & Robinson, D. H. (1999). Individual study, interactive multimedia, or cooperative learning: Which activity best supplements lecture-based distance education? *Journal of Educational Psychology, 91*(1), 169-174.

Bunn, M. D., & Barnes, R. E. (1999). Market segmentation for improved distance education program planning. *Distance Education, 20*(2), 274-294.

Carr, K. C., Fullerton, J. T., Severino, R., & McHugh, M. K. (1996). Barriers to completion of a nurse-midwifery distance education program. *Journal of Distance Education, 11*(1), 111-131.

Carr, S. (2000, February 11). As distance education comes of age, the challenge is keeping the students. *Chronicle of Higher Education, 46*(23), A39-A41.

Chyung, Y., Winiecki, D. J., & Fenner, J. A. (1998). A case study: Increase enrollments by reducing dropout rates in adult distance education. In *Distance learning '98: Proceedings of the annual conference on distance teaching and learning.* Madison: University of Wisconsin. (14th annual conference, Madison, WI, August 5-7, 1998)

Dirr, P. J. (1999, December). *Putting principles into practice: Promoting effective support services for students in distance learning programs: A report on the findings of a survey.* (Available from the Western Cooperative for Educational Telecommunications, P.O. Box 9752, Boulder, CO 80301)

Fjortoft, N. F. (1996). Persistence in a distance learning program: A case in pharmaceutical education. *American Journal of Distance Education, 10*(3), 49-59.

Greer, L. B., Hudson, L., & Paugh, R. (1998, October). *Student support services and success factors for adult on-line learners.* Paper presented at the annual conference of the International Society for the Exploration of Teaching Alternatives, Cocoa Beach, FL.

Johnson, D. W., Johnson, R. T., & Smith, K. A. (1991). *Active learning: Cooperation in the college classroom.* Edina, MN: Interaction Book Company.

Johnson, J. L. (1997, September). Commuter college students: What factors determine who will persist and who will drop out? *College Student Journal, 31*, 323-332.

Lords, E. (2000, May 19). Community colleges turn to consultants to help them recruit and retain students. *Chronicle of Higher Education, 46*(37), A65-A66.

Luedtke, C. B. (1999). *Distance education programs in Texas community and technical colleges: Assessing student support services in a virtual environment.* Unpublished master's thesis, Southwest Texas State University, San Marcos.

McCollum, K. (1997, October 10). Two universities put a chat-room program to an academic purpose. *Chronicle of Higher Education, 44*, A27.

McElhinney, J., & Nasseh, B. (1998-1999). Technical and pedagogical challenges faced by faculty and students in computer-based distance education in higher education in the United States. *Journal of Educational Technology, 27*(4), 349-359.

Menlove, R., Hansford, D., & Lignugaris-Kraft, B. (2000). Creating a community of distance learners: Putting technology to work. In *Capitalizing on leadership in rural special education: Making a difference for children and families.* Manhattan, KS: American Council on Rural Special Education. (Proceedings of the 20th annual conference, Alexandria, VA, March 16-18, 2000)

Morley, L., & LaMaster, K. J. (1999). Use electronic bulletin boards to extend classrooms. *Journal of Physical Education, Recreation and Dance, 70*(6), 16-18.

National Education Association. (2000, June). *A survey of traditional and distance learning higher education members.* Washington, DC: Author.

Parker, A. (1995). Distance education attrition. *International Journal of Educational Telecommunications, 1*(4), 389-406.

Reisberg, L. (1999, October 8). Colleges struggle to keep would-be dropouts enrolled. *Chronicle of Higher Education, 46*(7), A54-A56.

Schwitzer, A., & Lovell, C. (1999). Effects of goal instability, peer affiliation, and teacher support on distance learners. *Journal of College Student Development, 40*(1), 43-53.

Shale, D., & Gomes, J. (1998). Performance indicators and university distance education providers. *Journal of Distance Education, 13*(1), 1-20.

Terrell, S. R., & Dringus, L. (1999-2000). An investigation of the effect of learning style on student success in an online learning environment. *Journal of Educational Technology Systems, 28*(3), 231-238.

Wisely, N., & Jorgensen, M. (2000, Spring). Retaining students through social interaction: Special assignment residence halls. *Journal of College Admission, 167,* 16-28.

Zajkowski, M. E. (1993). Business students learning at a distance: One form of pre-enrollment counseling and its effect on retention. *Distance Education, 14*(2), 331-353.

9

Assessing Learning Outcomes

Assessment serves valuable purposes for both instructors and students. It provides students with appropriate, focused, and timely feedback to promote learning, keeps them informed regarding the progress they are making, and helps determine the extent to which they have achieved the outcomes of the course as a whole. For instructors, assessment is a good vehicle for communicating their goals to students so that they can learn more effectively, a means of identifying student misunderstandings and difficulties to guide instruction, and a source of information needed to assign student grades. In addition, assessment can deepen instructors' understanding of how students learn, thereby enhancing their competence to offer distance courses.

Distance education programs use a large variety of strategies to assist learners in achieving intended outcomes and to assess their progress. Learning outcomes are assessed in ways that are relevant to the program content, characteristics and situation of the learner, and the delivery system. Although assessment may be conducted to make judgments about an individual student, a given course, or an entire program, our discussion in this chapter will focus on procedures that measure or describe performance of individual students. In Chapter 10, we will shift our focus from individuals to courses or programs and will discuss methods used to answer questions regarding their operations, their effectiveness, and their efficiency.

Assessment in distance learning is both similar to and different from that used in on-campus programs. Because many useful resources are available for assessment in on-campus courses, this chapter focuses on aspects of assessment that are especially relevant for distance education courses. In these courses, assessment and measurement of student learning become even more critical in the absence of face-to-face interactions that enable instructors to use informal observations to gauge student response to instruction, to provide feedback on a regular basis, and to monitor student progress toward stated goals and objectives. Thus, instructors can use a variety of assessment approaches to monitor each learner's progress and to provide customized feedback to the learner at various points during the course. Accommodation of the special needs, characteristics, and situations of each learner becomes an important challenge for distance education instructors.

Although it is beneficial to conduct assessment throughout the course, this must be balanced against the instructor's workload and available time. As we noted in our discussion of good practices (Chapter 3), instructors need to plan carefully the number and the nature of assessment strategies that they will use, the level of detail that they will include in the feedback they provide, and the time between the assessments submitted by the learners. Students also appreciate having this information as a part of the course syllabus because this helps them plot their workloads at different points in the course. As we have emphasized throughout the book, distance education instructors must plan ahead, be highly creative and organized, and communicate with learners in new ways.

Guiding Principles

Before discussing the specific approaches to evaluating student performance, it is appropriate to outline principles guiding student assessment and mention some representative practices that provide specific examples of how a given principle might be implemented. Some of these principles and practices are not limited to distance education courses; many of them apply to on-campus courses as well, reflecting the premise that "good assessment is good assessment," regardless of whether the focus is on-campus or distance learning (Ragan, 1998).

Principle 1: Assessment instruments and activities should match the goals and objectives of the course.

Effective assessment begins with clear goals. Before teachers can assess how well the students are learning, they must identify and clarify outcomes that they want their students to achieve. The learning outcomes should be described in observable, measurable, and achievable terms; the learning design should be consistent with and shaped to help students achieve the intended outcomes; and assessment procedures should measure learner progress by reference to these outcomes (American Council on Education, 1996).

Several outcomes taxonomies are available to help conceptualize the outcomes for a course. The taxonomy of educational objectives developed by Bloom and his associates (1956) classifies outcomes relative to knowledge, comprehension, application, analysis, synthesis, and evaluation. A simple yet useful general typology has been developed by Ewell (1987), who suggests four basic dimensions of outcomes: (a) knowledge (both breadth and depth) outcomes; (b) skill outcomes (including basic, higher-order, and career-related skills); (c) attitudes and values outcomes; and (d) behavioral outcomes. One of these or similar taxonomies will help teachers organize the learning activities, select the media and the delivery system, design the assessment procedures, monitor students' progress, and assess their achievement in the course.

Learners appreciate having assessment and measurement strategies clearly communicated at the start of the course. Indeed, it is only fair to clearly state the nature, duration, due date, and impact on course grade of all assessment methods used in the course. Given the wide range of differences in characteristics, life experiences, and employment settings of learners enrolled in distance courses, it is useful to provide assessment options that capitalize on their unique characteristics and situations. For example, students can be given the option of conducting an applied project that helps them achieve the selected outcomes of the course and at the same time allows them to make a significant contribution in their place of employment.

In a distance learning course on social science research methods that one of us offers, students design and administer a questionnaire in an area of their interest, conduct the analysis of data they collect, and prepare a written report. This engages students in active learning, stimulates them to draw on their existing knowledge and understanding, helps them develop new skills of inquiry and interpretation, and allows them to make a worthwhile contribution in their work setting.

Principle 2: Assessment strategies should be an integral part of students' learning experience.

Assessment is more than a means of assigning grades. It is also an aid to facilitating learning for teachers as well as students. An important implication of this perspective has to do with designing and using assessment methods that are embedded in the curriculum and are, therefore, administered on a continuing basis. This approach may include (a) self-check quizzes presented online, in print materials, and in videotaped presentations; (b) comprehension tests included at the ends of sections within a topic area; and (c) application exercises, case studies, or simulations that are embedded at various points in the instructional materials and invite the learners to apply their newly acquired knowledge and understandings.

Available technology such as WebCT, Blackboard, and WebAssign can be used creatively to administer the assessment measures and provide immediate feedback to learners, thus creating milestones of accomplishment that help the learners grow toward the expected outcomes. Providing learners with continuing opportunities to monitor their learning and to assess if the assigned learning activity is working has the potential to stimulate learner-to-learner and learner-to-teacher interactions. In addition, technology such as WebCT and Blackboard can also provide learners with remedial loops and enrichment materials on a personalized basis. Depending on one's teaching philosophy, data from curriculum-embedded assessment may be used as a small contribution toward course grades as well.

In short, assessment should occur continuously. Students appreciate using such assessments to gauge their progress in the comfort of privacy. It allows them to monitor if they are learning effectively, provides feedback to confirm their understanding and to correct their misunderstandings, sustains their motivation to continue learning, and gives them continuing opportunities to practice self-assessment.

Principle 3: A variety of technologies and media should be considered to administer the assessment instruments and to obtain students' responses.

In Chapter 6, we discussed selecting appropriate technologies to facilitate student learning and to make distance education courses widely accessible. The technologies used to assess student learning are related to the delivery system(s) chosen. This, of course, is also related to what technology is available to students enrolled in the course. For a given technology, a range of options is available to administer assessment measures. For example, if all the students have access to computers, fax, and videotape players, how can each of those technologies be effectively used to administer various types of assessments? Furthermore, each of these technologies can be used in a number of ways. For example, a course bulletin board may be used for posting course assignments and discussion questions. Electronic mail and fax may be used to receive students' assignments and to provide them with individualized feedback in return. We also have used e-mail to communicate the grades that students have received on a proctor-administered exam and to provide students with comments related to the assignments they have submitted and the exams they have taken. One of our colleagues has used videotapes to assess students' oral presentations and counseling skills at several points during the course or in the program as a whole. Similarly, the telephone can be used to assess students' pronunciation in foreign language courses and to provide them with feedback.

Several media should be considered to assess student learning because each is effective for different purposes. For example, e-mail allows students to describe subjects, online chats or telephone interviews may work well to discuss the given topic, and video recordings may be used to demonstrate oral presentation skills or nonverbal interactions.

Principle 4: The integrity of assessment must be ensured.

Although security remains a concern in all courses and programs, this is especially true in distance education. Is the student actually doing the work? Is the work being done under the conditions specified by the instructor? One possible approach to ensure adequate security is to reduce the need and desire to cheat. This approach implies getting to know the learner better and creating a desirable, exciting learning environment wherein the learner wants and is able to achieve course outcomes without feeling the need to cheat (Hudspeth, 1999). Having learner-instructor discussions regarding the expected outcomes, their relevance, and the means for achieving them creates an atmosphere in which the learner becomes even more interested than the instructor in using multiple methods that effectively assess and document the progress toward and achievement of specified outcomes. Indeed, in such circumstances, a traditional multiple-choice or essay final exam may not be appropriate. Under some circumstances, however, it may still be necessary to ensure integrity by incorporating appropriate safeguards for protecting assessment instruments, and when required, proctoring exams. One of us has successfully used proctors in students' home communities to administer the exams under the specified conditions; the completed tests are mailed directly to the instructor by the proctor in the return envelope provided for this purpose. We recommend using equivalent forms of exams generated from item banks to minimize the likelihood of cheating during test administration.

Given the widespread availability of class notes and course-related material on the World Wide Web,[1] it is critical to pay special attention to potential plagiarism as well (Gibelman, Gelman, & Fast, 1999). We offer the following suggestions to prevent plagiarism: (a) Create assignments that are judged by the learners to be relevant to the outcomes they perceive as useful and desirable; (b) make sure that the suggested resources have been assessed for availability, currency, and usability; (c) provide feedback on the assignment outline before students start working on the assignment itself; and (d) make unexpected phone calls to discuss a point further or to ask the student how he or she found some piece of information.

As we noted in Chapter 4, the course syllabus should include a policy regarding cheating and plagiarism. Explaining what plagiarism is and indicating that it is a serious offense may not only prevent the naive student from committing unintentional plagiarism but also deter the intentional plagiarists. Students should be advised that the instructor plans to do random checks for plagiarism by using technology available for this purpose (for example, www.plagiarism.org/). In other words, although technology provides students new and easier ways to cheat, it also offers the instructors easier ways to catch cheaters.

Principle 5: The quality of the assessment process should be monitored.

However good we are at assessing student learning, we also learn from assessing the assessment, monitoring its effectiveness, and keeping a watch on what works and what does not. Such monitoring includes (a) checking the assessment methods for internal validity and reliability, (b) ensuring that the methods are appropriate in a distance learning environment, and (c) determining whether all the assessment methods are really necessary and whether it is possible to combine some of them or delete others.

What approaches can be used to monitor the quality of the assessment processes? Although the effectiveness of monitoring approaches may depend on the course, its delivery system, and the assessment procedures, here are some strategies that we have found helpful.

Keep notes from year to year. These notes may include information regarding the timing of assessment, difficulties of interpretation, and the time it took to examine students' work and to provide feedback. These notes can be used to design better assessment tools when the course is next offered.

Invite students to give feedback on the quality of assessment. This may include asking students questions such as "Am I giving you enough feedback?" "Does this exercise promote learning?" "Are graded assignments returned fast enough for you?" "In what ways can I improve the assessment processes?" "How clear are the instructions for different assignments?" Such feedback can be (and probably should be) secured throughout the course, not just at the end.

Examine student performance data on various elements of assessment. Such data can be used to identify areas in which students generally showed strengths and weaknesses. This information may be helpful in making adjustments in instructional design as well as in the assessment procedures.

Use postcourse assessment instruments. This approach is useful in obtaining student input regarding instructional design, delivery system, and assessment methods. Although this information becomes available at the end of the course, it still can be useful for making changes when the course is next offered.

It is also good to do an end-of-the-course reflection on what the instructor wanted the students to learn and to what degree the assessment procedures helped determine the extent to which the students achieved the intended outcomes. Appropriately designed course evaluations from students also provide valuable information in this regard.

Methods of Assessment

As we have emphasized throughout the chapter, an effective assessment design includes multiple measures taken through time. Employing a wide range of assessment methods allows students to do their best on measures that match their styles, strengths, and preferences and minimizes the likelihood of penalizing students who happen to be weak in responding to one or two forms of assessment. An additional factor contributing to the design of assessment methods concerns their purpose: Methods to provide diagnostic feedback are different from those designed to determine end-of-course achievement of intended outcomes. In contrast to assessment conducted at the end of the course, methods used to provide diagnostic feedback have a more narrowly defined focus, concentrating on highly specific content knowledge or skills. They are generally designed to provide an analysis of learners' particular strengths and weaknesses, to suggest causes for their difficulties, and to offer recommendations regarding instructional needs and available resources.

This section presents selected approaches relevant for assessing learning outcomes in distance courses. This presentation builds on the good practices in distance education outlined in Chapter 3. Indeed, effective assessment methods should enhance student learning and, at the same time, provide the instructors with information they need to monitor and grade student progress.

Group Discussions

Learning is an active process. As we commented in Chapter 3, many instructors use technology to help students move from a passive to an active mode of learning. Engaging students in discussing the key topics or issues on a weekly basis enhances their learning and keeps them feeling connected with each other and with the instructor. In a Web-based course on aging and diversity that one of us offers, all students are required to participate in asynchronous discussion each week. Of the total course grade, 30% depends on students' contribution to the questions or the activity the instructor posts in the course conference area each week. The instructor monitors the group discussion, reviews the themes that surface, and notes the misconceptions and the difficulties that students may have with regard to a given topic. In addition, with the help of available technology, the instructor also tracks who participates in the discussion and who does not. At the end of the week, the instructor brings closure to the discussion by synthesizing the key points presented by the students and by providing clarification or explanation in areas in which students may have experienced difficulty.

In short, networked discussion groups draw together students from different backgrounds and settings; engage them in energetic, productive conversations; allow students to maintain contact with the instructor and classmates; and provide the teacher with a documented record of the quality of each student's contribution, which may be used for assessment purposes. Such discussions stimulate students to think about what they have read and heard and to share their reactions without worrying about interrupting others.

The Student Log or Journal

Asking students to keep a log or journal engages them in self-reflection and self-evaluation, stimulates them to think about what they have read and experienced, and gives them additional practice in writing. The purpose of such writing is not for the students to summarize what they are reading but to note their reactions, questions, comments, criticisms, and insights. Research evidence indicates that journals, as well as other writing, produce gains in learning, thinking, and motivation (Hettich, 1990).

Many instructors do not grade journals, given the personal nature of the writing and the variability in the content that students focus on, how they connect the writing with experiences outside the course, and the level of details they decide to provide. Instead, the instructor may allocate a specific number of points for merely writing the journal. Keeping a journal for a given course or an entire program provides students with concrete evidence regarding the gains they have achieved in their quality of thinking and writing. It is reasonable to assume that the active observation, self-reflection, and self-assessment carry over to other courses and work life. As we had indicated in our discussion of diagnostic learning logs in Chapter 3, student journals can provide the instructor with valuable insights and suggestions for improving instructional delivery. Instructors should make clear whether they will read the journal simply to verify that it was done or to assess quality of the reflection.

Because student logs are essentially another continuing assignment that requires time and effort from students and teachers, it is important to consider how their use complements other assessment methods employed in the course. Do the journals add a component that is significantly different from other parts of the assessment, or do they duplicate what is already being accomplished by other means of promoting self-reflection and self-assessment? In addition, consider how writing journals on a regular basis may help students achieve the outcomes envisioned for the course or the program.

Term Papers

Term papers provide students with opportunities to apply principles and generalizations from the course to new problems and situations, to synthesize and integrate information and ideas, to explore problems or to focus on areas of special significance to them, and to improve writing skills. Simply writing a paper and getting a letter grade at the end of the course, however, are not enough. Instead, students' learning is enhanced when (a) they write several short papers spread throughout the term rather than one long paper at the end of the term;

(b) they prepare a prospectus outlining what they want to focus on and how they plan to proceed; (c) they receive instructor analysis and feedback on the prospectus before they start working on the paper itself; and (d) they receive both the letter grade and instructor comments on the paper in a timely manner. Students can submit the prospectus electronically as a word processor file to the instructor. In turn, the teacher can provide comments and suggestions within the same file electronically and can answer questions the student may have as a result of developing the prospectus.

Our experience indicates that students like preparing shorter papers spread through time because this allows them to synthesize and integrate manageable chunks of information and ideas, gives them an opportunity to interact with the instructor at several points in the course, and gives them an indication of the progress they are making in achieving the course outcomes. Given the high level of anxiety many students experience regarding their final course grade, obtaining instructor feedback and marks on several short papers is less terrifying than waiting to receive a grade after writing one long paper at the end of the course. Another technique is to have students prepare short assignments or submit their work in installments, which are then integrated into a final paper at the end of the course. For example, different subtopics can be treated independently in short papers but then interconnected in the final term paper.

All students, especially distance learning students, appreciate receiving clear and detailed instructions regarding the paper(s) they are required to write. They like to know how much freedom they have with regard to the topic, form, content, purpose, and the like. They also like to know what style (APA, University of Chicago, Modern Language Association, etc.) they should use to provide citations and to write references. In addition, and perhaps more important, they appreciate knowing what criteria will be used to evaluate their papers and assign grades. Thus, instructors should develop guidelines that provide students with the information and structure they need to complete an assignment. Including clear instructions and timelines in the course syllabus also helps instructors communicate the expectations they have for the students who enroll in the course.

We have found that students benefit from developing a prospectus (or first draft) and receiving timely feedback before they begin substantial work on their papers. If this two-phase approach is used, instructors should provide students with specific directions for preparing the prospectus as well. Angelo and Cross (1993) have outlined the prompts that may be adapted to help students develop a prospectus for a paper. Distance students should be encouraged to include in the prospectus specific questions and concerns they would like addressed by the instructor. In addition to providing feedback on each student's prospectus, the instructor may also disseminate a summary list of suggestions based on all the drafts reviewed. This approach will help achieve considerable efficiency by minimizing the need of repeating similar comments to each learner. Preparing such a summary may also help in making modifications and revisions in the paper and/or prospectus guidelines for the next offering of the course.

Student Portfolios

Because distance education has the potential to accommodate the special needs, characteristics, and situations of each learner, portfolios present a useful assessment technique in documenting a learner's development throughout the course. Although there are many types of portfolios, each is a purposeful presentation of the work produced by a single learner through time. Well-conceived portfolios include samples representing both work in progress and showpiece samples and the students' reflections about their work and a discussion of how well it demonstrates progress toward and/or achievement of course outcomes. For example, to demonstrate the progress the learner has made, a portfolio might include the initial draft, a revision, and the final form of an assignment. Of course, technology has made it convenient for both learners and instructors to keep their work on file and assemble it for a purposeful presentation.

An important element of portfolios is the learners' explanations of their work in relation to the course outcomes and self-assessments of the progress achieved. Thus, this technique allows students to reflect on the development of their self-evaluative skills and promotes increased self-awareness. This, in turn, helps the instructors assess the extent to which students are able to make connections between their work and course outcomes. Looking at the progress they have made with regard to specified outcomes also has the potential to strengthen students' commitment to personal achievement.

In a master's program in education offered via distance learning at The College of St. Scholastica, all students develop portfolios as a part of their capstone experience. They are provided the following instructions:

> *Format.* You may submit portfolios which are paper or electronic, in whatever form you prefer (e.g., folder, binder). The possibilities are truly endless. Please be sure to include a table of contents, so that we don't lose our way in examining it. Remember each portfolio will be unique!
>
> *Content.* Review all course work you have completed, reflecting on your personal growth throughout the master's program. Develop a brief (not more than five pages) statement of personal growth, then in some way support the claims of growth you have made. This support may include written documentation or actual work samples or photos. Be as individual as you wish on this. Also include a professional plan for your continued growth and reflection. This might include topics you would like to explore, strategies you wish to implement, and the goals you would like to achieve.

In addition to the previous instructions for preparing a portfolio, the course syllabus includes the criteria to be used in assessing it. These criteria focus on (a) final statement of personal growth, (b) support for the final statement, and (c) projection of future growth.

Portfolios can also be used in conjunction with a learning contract defining what the instructor has proposed and what the learner has agreed to do. Although the written agreement clearly describes the outcomes to be demonstrated by the learner, it provides considerable flexibility regarding the means and methods that the learner may use to achieve them. Considering the large variety of learning resources available via the Internet and other media, it is unlikely that different learners will use the same resources and same methods to achieve the given outcomes. Therefore, it is even more important for students to explain how the pieces in their portfolios respond to the key topics and questions that the instructor included in the syllabus and to demonstrate how they made progress in achieving the stated outcomes.

Because students may have limited experience in developing a portfolio, we offer the following suggestions:

1. Provide learners with clearly stated guidelines or rules regarding portfolio content or form.

2. Provide instructions on format and length when asking students to write their commentary on the significance of the pieces they decide to include in the portfolio.

3. Offer ungraded feedback on the prospectus or the outline that students develop before they do substantive work on the portfolio.

4. Link the portfolio with other graded assignments (such as papers and project reports) included in the course.

5. Allow learners to use images, graphics, and tables, rather than prose alone. Students might include audiotapes, videotapes, and other artifacts along with the written narrative.

6. Clearly indicate the amount of course credit to be offered for the portfolio.

7. Alert students early in the course that substantial time is needed to prepare a portfolio.

8. Provide students the criteria that will be used in assessing their portfolios.

Tests

We have already indicated our belief that traditional forms of testing (multiple-choice, fill-in-the-blank, true-false, etc.) may be inappropriate tools for determining grades in a distance instruction program. Some testing methods, however, may be appropriate as an integral part of instructional design. They may be used to engage students in active learning, to help maintain their interest, and to give them opportunities to assess their own learning throughout the course. As we discuss in Chapter 10, such exams may also be necessary to establish equivalency with on-campus versions of the distance course. In addition, tests may also provide students with the experience they need to perform well in taking online professional exams after graduating from the distance program. One good example of using multiple-choice tests to stimulate student thinking is provided by Just-in-Time Teaching (Novak, Patterson, Gavrin, & Christian, 1999), a technique whereby students take multiple-choice tests before each class meeting. The test results alert students and their instructors to misconceptions and gaps in the learners' knowledge and understanding and help focus the discussion that will take place in a given class session. Such use of multiple-choice tests can also be adapted to distance learning programs: Students first are given a small number of test items to take and then are provided with the answer key as a part of the instructional package. Our experience indicates that such an approach works well both in Web-based and in video-based distance education courses.

Another version of these diagnostic tools is a self-administered test taken immediately after the learners have completed the given module to determine mastery of the material. Available technology such as WebCT then is used to evaluate students' responses and determine which module would best serve learner needs. In a way, this design of instruction and assessment is similar to what has been traditionally used in branched approaches to programmed learning that take into account the individual differences in students' ability to learn. Students may advance to a more difficult section of the material, skipping some modules, if they demonstrate mastery of the essentials of the topic at hand. If the students' mistakes indicate poor progress in learning the material, they can be directed to a different presentation of the same material for remedial assistance. The key point is that such an approach uses modular tests to assess students' mastery of the essentials and uses the information to direct the learners to the next module. All this, of course, is done with the help of available technology that records and analyzes students' responses automatically. Students receive immediate feedback on their progress and reinforcement for displaying mastery of the material.

If an end-of-course exam will be used to determine the extent to which students have achieved the outcomes envisioned for the course, we recommend using a mix of different types of questions to balance measurement of the intended outcomes. Such a mix could include problems, short-answer items, and essay topics. Designing several forms of the test helps ensure security of the test material and minimizes the likelihood of cheating during the exam. As we suggested in an earlier section of the chapter, students could be asked to identify local people (college personnel, clergy, or high school teachers) who can proctor exams; then the tests could be sent directly to the proctors with guidelines for administering and returning the tests. Although this approach has worked well for us, we recognize that it may be impractical for some programs if large numbers of proctors are needed or if reimbursement for proctors is required.

If objective tests (multiple-choice, true-false, and matching items) are to be used, commercially available software can generate multiple equivalent forms of an exam from a bank of questions the instructor has written. The software can scramble the order of questions or select a different group of items that assess the same outcomes. Another possibility is to use computer-adaptive testing (CAT), an approach currently used by the Educational Testing Service to administer admission tests such as the Graduate Record Examination and the Graduate Management Admissions Test. Typically, a CAT begins with medium difficulty questions but then tailors itself to each student's achievement level. Students who give correct answers are automatically given more difficult questions; conversely, incorrect answers beget easier questions. Because CAT individualizes the test items that a student is asked to answer, this approach minimizes the possibility of cheating. At the present time, however, CAT requires considerable technical support in assembling the item pool.

Conclusion

Distance learning programs attract students who differ significantly from each other in their learning styles, pace of learning, work experiences, and assessment preferences. Consequently, it is equally essential to provide students with choices in tasks (not all reading and writing) and options for demonstrating mastery or competence, to allow them time to contemplate and complete the assignments, and to offer them opportunities for revision and rethinking. Educators should avoid overusing timed exams. Students are likely to do better when they know the course goals, see models and examples of "good work," and know how their performance compares with the acceptable standards. Integrating assessment with instruction allows students to see the connection between their efforts and results and keeps them motivated to do well. Students will bring their rich life experience to the course; they appreciate opportunities to relate what they have recently learned to their personal experiences, prior knowledge, and new situations.

Summary Tips

- Use assessment instruments and activities that are congruent with the goals and objectives of the course.

- Clearly communicate the nature, duration, due date, and impact on the course grade of all planned assessment methods.

- Provide students with self-assessment opportunities by integrating assessment with instruction.

- Employ a variety of technologies and media to administer assessment instruments, to obtain students' responses, and to maintain needed records.

- Create an environment that makes the learning process so desirable and exciting that the students want to achieve the course outcomes without the need to cheat.

- Include in the course syllabus a policy regarding cheating and plagiarism.

- Develop proper safeguards for protecting assessment instruments and, when required, proctoring of exams.

- Design and use assessment methods that are perceived by the learners to be relevant to the stated outcomes.

- Monitor the assessment process by obtaining student input, examining student performance data, and keeping notes about how the assessment methods are working.

- Employ a wide range of assessment methods allowing students to do their best on the measures that match their styles, strengths, and preferences.

- Promote student-content, student-teacher, and student-student interaction through networked discussion groups, and use the record of students' participation and contribution for assessment purposes.

- Engage students in self-reflection and self-evaluation by asking them to keep a log or journal outlining their reactions, questions, comments, criticisms, and insights related to what they are experiencing in the course.

- Ask students to write several short papers spread throughout the course rather than one long paper at the end of the course.

- Provide students with clear and detailed instructions regarding the papers, projects, and portfolios required for the course.

- Offer individualized feedback to students on the outlines they develop for their papers before they start substantive work on the papers themselves.

- Invite students to develop portfolios to document their development with regard to the learning outcomes for the course or program.

- Make sure that the amount of assessment is appropriate; students' learning should not be impeded by an overload of assessing requirements, nor should the quality of teaching be impaired by excessive burdens of assessment-related tasks.

- Use a course evaluation form to obtain students' reactions to various aspects of the course.

WWW ➤   At our Sage Web site, www.sagepub.com/mehrotra

Our companion Web site includes specific examples of methods that we have found useful for assessing student learning in distance education courses. In addition, we include links to electronic resources pertaining to assessment of students' knowledge, skills, and attitudes.

Note

1. www.collegeclub.com/micro/versity/main.asp?id=, www.askanexpert.com, and www.webmath.com

References

American Council on Education. (1996). *Distance learning evaluation guide*. Washington, DC: Author.

Angelo, T. A., & Cross, K. P. (1993). *Classroom assessment techniques: A handbook for college teachers* (2nd ed.). San Francisco: Jossey-Bass.

Bloom, B. S. (Ed.) and others. (1956). *Taxonomy of educational objectives: The classification of educational goals: Handbook I. Cognitive domain.* New York: Longmans, Green.

Ewell, P. (1987). Establishing a campus-based program assessment. In D. F. Halpern (Ed.), *Student outcomes assessment: What institutions stand to gain* (New Directions for Higher Education, No. 59, pp. 9-24). San Francisco: Jossey-Bass.

Gibelman, M., Gelman, S., & Fast, J. (1999, Fall). The downside of cyberspace: Cheating made easy. *Journal of Social Work Education, 35*(3), 367-376.

Hettich, P. (1990). Journal writing: Old fare or nouvelle cuisine? *Teaching of Psychology, 17,* 36-39.

Hudspeth, D. (1999). Testing learner outcomes in Web-based instruction. In B. H. Khan (Ed.), *Web-based instruction* (pp. 353-356). Englewood Cliffs, NJ: Educational Technology.

Novak, G. M., Patterson, E. T., Gavrin, A. D., & Christian, W. (1999). *Just-in-time teaching: Blending active learning with Web technology.* Upper Saddle River, NJ: Prentice Hall.

Ragan, L. C. (1998). Good teaching is good teaching: An emerging set of guiding principles and practices for the design and development of distance education [Online]. *DEOSNEWS, 8*(12). Retrieved April 2, 2001, from the World Wide Web: www.ed.psu.edu/ACSDE

10

Program Evaluation

In Chapter 9, we focused on assessing the performance of individual students to create a picture of their learning that they can use to improve their performance and that the institution can use to document their achievement. We now go from the individual level to the course or program level, where information from individuals is aggregated to summarize a group's progress and to draw conclusions about a program's effectiveness. Here, *group* may refer to any of a wide variety of student aggregations, such as at the course, group of courses, or program level, or to students grouped by sex, race/ethnicity, class year, major, place of residence, delivery mode, and so on.

At any level of aggregation, the focus is on the program (or the course) rather than on the individual learner, and the overarching goal of this evaluation is to ensure the delivery of high-quality instruction to the target population. Just as assessment of individual students leads to improved learning by providing feedback and guidance at several points, program evaluation contributes to improved instruction by providing detailed feedback regarding input, processes, and outcomes

173

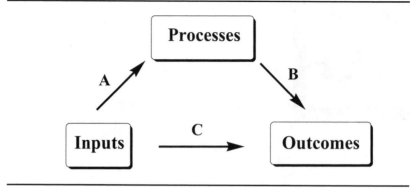

Figure 10.1. The I-P-O Model

to those who can make changes or programmatic decisions. In other words, evaluation may be conducted to gauge program effectiveness where it is intended to be (a) formative, facilitating program modification and enhancing the achievement of extended outcomes, and (b) summative, providing information to support a judgement about the program's worth, so that a decision can be made about the merit of its continuation.

Although there are many similarities between student assessment and program evaluation, there are some important differences as well. To help identify these differences, we have presented a conceptual framework in Figure 10.1.

Program evaluation is incomplete unless it includes information on program inputs, learning processes, and student outcomes.

- *Inputs* refer to characteristics of the learners and the instructional methods.

- *Processes* represent what the learners actually do during the course or the program.

- *Outcomes* refer to the impacts of what learners did.

As we remarked earlier, the focus in Chapter 9 was mainly on outcomes. Assessment of individual students' outcomes allows instructors to give them feedback and to document their achievement. In program evaluation, we focus on each of the three boxes shown in Figure 10.1 and how well they are functioning together.

In a distance learning program, inputs may refer to (a) students' attributes such as their prior knowledge, experience, attitudes, level of commitment, and self-motivation; and (b) program characteristics such as instructional methods, technologies, library resources, and instructional staff. Program processes represent activities such as (a) learners' interaction with the content, the instructor, and other learners; (b) how often they work on the assignments, what they actually do, and what feedback they receive and how they use it; and (c) what support services they use and how often they use them in areas such as library, instruction, technology, advising, and counseling. Program outcomes refer to student achievement and attitudes, drop-out rates, completion rates, and student satisfaction with the program. Traditionally, evaluation has focused on the relationship shown by Arrow B in Figure 10.1— the effect of processes on outcome variables. Experience indicates, however, that the relationship between processes and outcomes cannot be understood without taking into account program inputs. Program inputs (e.g., student characteristics, for example) may be related to both outcomes (Arrow C) and processes (Arrow A). In other words, differences among students tend to show some consistency through time (Arrow C), and different types of students often select and use different types of programs (distance learning, traditional on-campus classes) and instructional strategies (Arrow A). That inputs are thus related to both outputs and processes means that inputs can, in turn, affect the observed relationship between the program processes and outputs (Astin, 1991).

The key point is that the model presented in Figure 10.1 includes the assessment not only of student learning but also of student and program characteristics and the learning processes. Thus, by looking at inputs, processes, and outcomes, program evaluation leads to a better understanding of why certain outcomes are not being achieved. Simply examining outcomes of distance programs is not adequate. We should focus on input and processes as well. Why? Because this approach allows us to interpret outcome data, to help understand for whom the program works and for whom it does not, and to make needed improvements. In addition, input and process evaluation provides useful information for dissemination of an effective program and its use by others.

Evaluating Program Inputs

It is difficult, if not impossible, to ascertain how a distance learning program affects students' outcomes in the absence of data regarding the characteristics of the students and the learning design. Although the most obvious use of student input data is as a pretest of student outcome measures, it can be used for other purposes as well. For example, developing a profile of learner characteristics such as ethnicity, place of residence, work experience, attitudes toward distance learning, and self-motivation can be helpful in understanding the program's recruitment and admissions efforts and in predicting achievement and satisfaction level of the learner. This information can also help identify factors that may be affecting prospective students' decisions to engage in a distance learning program. In addition, information on attributes of entering students may assist in tracking their progress, in monitoring program implementation, and in conducting program review. Finally, a comprehensive profile of the students entering a program provides excellent material for use in public addresses by program officials and press releases to local, regional, and national media.

Input data serve a wide range of purposes, but how are such data collected? The following section presents some examples of methods useful in collecting data on student attributes relevant for evaluating distance programs.

The Application Form

Obtaining biographical information from the applicants has both intuitive and intrinsic validity because it speaks directly to a central measurement axiom, namely, what a person will do in the future is best predicted from what he or she has done in the past. In distance education programs offered by The College of St. Scholastica, faculty have found it useful to ask the interested learners to complete an application form that includes a variety of questions focusing on demographic, experiential, and attitudinal variables related to success in a distance program. Applicants describe their educational experiences, work history, computer-related skills, access to a library, work habits, management skills, attitude toward distance learning, and commitment to the program.

Although it is important to review available research on student characteristics correlated with success in distance programs (for example, Powell, Conway, & Ross, 1990), we suggest that a form be tailored to obtain the needed information regarding the applicants interested in a particular course or program. The variables that others have used may serve as a starting point in designing an application form that can provide the information specific to the program. It is beneficial to monitor how well the application form meets its intended purpose, what difficulties are experienced by the applicants in completing various items, and what changes will make the form easier to understand.

The Application Essay

Given the heavy emphasis on written assignments in many distance programs, applicants may be invited to submit a two-page essay on a topic related to the program content and delivery mode. In one master of education program that uses videotapes, print materials, and on-campus meetings, the program director asks each applicant to submit an essay describing why he or she wants to enroll in the program, what objectives the prospective student would like to achieve, and how the program fits with the applicant's career plans. Preliminary analysis indicated that a careful review of the essays allows the admissions committee to assess an applicant's reasoning ability, writing skills, level of motivation, and expectations of the program. Application essays also have been useful in assessing the progress that students make as a result of their participation in the program: Comparing their own writing at several points in the program helps students perform a self-assessment and enables them to pinpoint areas in which additional work is needed.

In addition to the application forms and essays, data on students' input are obtained by examining their grade records and by administering pretests directly related to the focus of the course. As we observed earlier, keeping pretest data on file to compare with posttest data represents a common approach to assessing program effectiveness. Like other information from student input data, pretest results may be helpful in developing a better understanding of factors correlated with student success in the program.

So far in this section, our discussion has focused on student characteristics. We now proceed to discuss program characteristics, which also critically affect the outcomes of a given program.

Program Characteristics

In the broadest sense, program characteristics include everything that may happen to students during the program and may conceivably influence the outcomes under consideration. Because distance education programs vary considerably in areas such as intended outcomes, learning design, technology delivery mode, and learner support, it is essential to create a detailed description of program characteristics. Identifying key characteristics helps the instructor conceptualize what aspect of the program is intended to have an effect on student learning and articulate how the program compares with the corresponding on-campus program. Paying close attention to essential details helps the evaluator understand what the program aims to achieve, its goals, how it works, and what resources it uses. This information is later employed to monitor the learning process, to understand the data, to interpret the meaning of outcome data, to make recommendations, and to report the evaluation findings. Information about the program is useful both for current and future participants. For example, potential participants would like to know what delivery mode will be used, what type of computer will be needed (if any), what modes and level of interaction with classmates and the instructors are anticipated, what assessment procedures will be used, and what support will be available in areas such as technology, library, advising, and counseling.

Perhaps the best approach to collecting information about program characteristics is to carefully examine all the materials available regarding the course. Examples include *print materials*, such as a copy of the college or program catalog, course syllabi, study guides, and textbooks and readings; and *electronic materials*, such as program or course Web sites, which may include information regarding the instructor(s) responsible for the course, students enrolled in the course, the course bulletin board or conference area, and procedures regarding lecture notes, grade posting, and schedule changes.

If program evaluation is conducted by external evaluators, they may find it beneficial to (a) conduct interviews with students and those responsible for designing and offering the course, (b) compare the course with selected similar courses offered in traditional or distance programs, and (c) examine the course design with regard to its potential to engage students in active learning and help them maintain contact with the instructor.

Because many evaluations contrast the effects of different formats of distance learning and on-campus programs, it follows that data on both student characteristics and program characteristics will be collected from all programs to be included for comparison. This means that data collection methods used by the evaluators should have the sensitivity to capture the key features of all programs under consideration and the specific characteristics of the students they serve. This information will be useful in interpreting data on outcomes achieved in each case and will help in identifying similarities and differences among programs.

Program Processes

Labels are not programs. All distance education programs with the same titles are not similar. Even when the course syllabi, the announced outcomes, and the delivery mode look identical, courses may differ from each other in how they are implemented. Simply stated, there is no substitute for gathering actual data on what happens in each program and who does what and when. Thus, rather than taking program titles and names at face value or looking at the course materials, it is essential to examine how the program actually operates. The goal of such examination is to assess fidelity of the program to what was presented in the catalog and/or the syllabus and to answer questions such as these: What do the learners actually do? How often do they interact with each other and why? What support services do they use and why? How do the students experience and perceive various aspects of the program? Thus, this phase of evaluation places an emphasis on looking at how a product or outcome is produced, rather than simply looking at the product or the outcome in isolation. Examining the process as well as the outcomes provides an analysis of the ways a program produces the results it achieves. Gathering data on what the instructors and the learners actually did and how well they did it helps detect or predict defects in the program design, the delivery system, and the instructional materials; provides information for program decisions; and contributes to developing records of how the program actually operates.

The range of individual differences in the characteristics of students enrolled in distance programs (such as learning styles, self-study skills, and motivation) should prompt the reviewer to focus on how individuals learn, rather than describing only how groups learn. An important way of monitoring the process through time is to establish a management information system. This approach provides continuing data in areas such as students' characteristics, their frequency of participation in each of the activities, their use of library or other support services, their reaction to program assignments, and program costs. Although this approach to program monitoring has considerable potential, it is difficult to design a useful system for a given program and ensure that it is actually used. Our experience with program evaluation indicates that in comparison with outcome assessment, considerably less attention has been given to process monitoring. Advances in computer technology and the availability of software such as WebCT and Blackboard, however, cause us to believe that process evaluation can be accomplished effectively and efficiently and that the evaluation results can advance the process of understanding why students do well in certain programs and not so well in others.

If the program is offered via ITV at one or more sites, structured observation may be used to collect data about specific behaviors of the instructors and the students. For example, classroom observers can attend a 50-minute class and record the number of times a given instructor performed each of the behaviors related to good practices in undergraduate education. For each site, the observers can record the numbers of questions students raised, the number of students who became engaged in discussion, or any other observable behavior that is relevant to the evaluation of the program under review. If the audio or video recordings of the sessions become available, the evaluator can view them at a later date and code them to capture the types of interactions that occurred, their order, their frequency, and so on.

Systematic observation is a valuable approach when the evaluation needs to focus on areas such as specific behaviors, interactions, nonverbal communications, and classroom climate in one or more sites. It may provide information about behavior patterns that may not be obtained by self-reporting, a management information system, or other methods.

In the previous chapter, we included a description of student logs or journals as an approach to assessing student learning and monitoring how they react to various aspects of the course. Aggregating such information for a course or a program can provide unique insights into program processes as experienced and understood by different segments of the student population. Similarly, an analysis of the portfolios developed by students enrolled in a given program can help evaluators understand what students actually did, how they did it, what worked, and what did not work.

Finally, information about program processes and the use of instructional technologies can be obtained by designing student surveys that focus on program elements such as learning design, objectives and outcomes, materials, technologies, and support. Depending on the purpose, such surveys can be conducted for specific courses while students are enrolled in the program and for the program as a whole after they have graduated. We have found that comments from program alumni provide thoughtful perspectives that assist in making significant changes and adjustments in the program.

In summary, it is essential to use multiple methods to create a developmental picture of how the program actually operates, how the different technologies work together, what the instructors and learners do at different points in the program, what learning resources they use, and what difficulties they encounter and how they resolve them. Preparing such a detailed explanation of the learning process helps in making program modifications and adjustments, in understanding students' progress in achieving the learning outcomes, and in disseminating the program for widespread use. In the next section, we devote our attention to a discussion of assessing program outcomes.

Assessing Outcomes

Of the three classes of evaluation variables presented in Figure 10.1, outcomes are generally the most critical and important to students, instructors, and administrators. In essence, outcomes refer to those aspects of students' development that the program does influence or attempts to influence through instruction. Examples of program outcomes include student achievement, retention, and satisfaction. Because the issue of cost or the effort required to achieve a given magnitude of desired change is implicit in all outcome evaluations, we will also include a discussion of relating costs to program results. This information informs decisions about allocation of resources, facilitates comparisons between the distance program and a traditional on-campus program, and helps garner support of administrators who determine the fate of new programs and services.

Student Learning

In Chapter 9, we outlined guiding principles and methods useful in assessing the performance of individual students. In conducting a program evaluation, the data collected for individual students are aggregated for a course, for a program, and for a delivery mode depending on the nature of questions under investigation. A gentle reminder: *The purpose is to make conclusions about a given program, rather than about an individual student.* Because the program impact may not be similar for each of the intended outcomes, we suggest that the analysis be conducted separately for each outcome. Results of this analysis provide diagnostic information about various aspects of the program and may direct the instructor(s) to make changes and adjustments necessary to strengthen student learning. This information may be used to review the learning outcomes, thereby ensuring their clarity, utility, and appropriateness.

In addition to outcomes involving knowledge and skills, program evaluation needs to include affective outcomes as well: students' feelings, attitudes, values, beliefs, self-concepts, aspirations, and social and interpersonal relationships. Although the number of these outcomes is large, techniques for their assessment are not as far advanced as those for cognitive outcomes. Because distance instruction is often criticized for not devoting adequate attention to the development of affective outcomes, we suggest that such outcomes be included in designing instructional strategies, in monitoring the program processes, and in assessing their effectiveness. At a minimum, outcome assessment should include some self-administered questionnaires and inventories that focus on student attitudes, values, and interpersonal relationships and skills. Regardless of the procedures used to assess how the distance program affects the learners, it is essential to ensure that the procedures meet the requirements of reliability and validity.

Student Retention

Concern about the drop-out rate in distance education (Merisotis, 1999) has prompted an increasing number of programs to use retention rate as an outcome measure. This assumes that the information provides an indication of the learners' dissatisfaction with the program. It also may indicate characteristics of the program that militate against full participation. Finally, it may also indicate the lack of match between the learner style and preference with the program design and the delivery mode. Because many distance programs provide students with flexibility regarding when they can enter and when they can graduate, it is important to make sure that the categories such as *acceptance, absence, completion,* and *departure* are purposeful and valid. Developing an operational definition of these categories will provide numbers that are credible and useful. In other words, careful thought must be given to determine how the numbers and rates will be calculated, how they will be used, and how they will be communicated. Once the program staff agree on the operational definitions of the relevant categories, it is wise to keep the definitions on file to ensure consistency in their use through time. Without such consistency, the rates calculated at different points will not be comparable.

Simply calculating the retention rate is not enough. If the overarching goal of evaluation is program improvement, follow-up studies are needed to investigate why some learners persist and others drop out. It is beneficial to identify characteristics that distinguish between the two groups of learners. Such analysis may guide changes in the recruitment and selection procedures as well as modifications in learning design, mode of instructional delivery, and student support.

How can data on students who drop out from the program be collected? Because learners' characteristics are a major factor in outcome achievement and satisfaction with the program, the starting point should be an examination of existing data on students' attributes. Data sources include the application materials, records of completed work in a single course or many courses, faculty notes and comments regarding their work, records on the learners' interactions with others enrolled in the program, and the pattern of how they have used various resources. Another approach is to design a short questionnaire, send it electronically, and give respondents the option of replying by U.S. mail or e-mail. If an existing questionnaire is used, it should be adapted to the specific program's needs. Students prefer short questionnaires and those that allow them to remain anonymous.

Learner Satisfaction

We have already commented on the drop-out rate as an indicator of learner dissatisfaction with the program. In addition to examining the drop-out rate, the retention rate, and the completion rate in a given course or a program, it is also important to gather data regarding the satisfaction of learners with various aspects of the distance program. Such data may be collected at the end of each course and at the end of the program. In a master's program in education offered by The College of St. Scholastica via distance learning, satisfaction data are collected 6 months after students have graduated from the program. A discussion of the survey questions and the key findings may be found in the North Central Association of Colleges and Schools proceedings (Mehrotra, 1999). Experience indicated that such follow-up surveys allow the alumni to reflect on their experience in the program, to make comparisons with graduates of other programs, and to examine the extent to which the program helped them develop knowledge, attitudes, and skills they need to succeed in their work settings.

When satisfaction data are collected at several points during and after learners' participation in the program, it is important to identify when such data were collected, who was included, who was not included, and what aspects of the program or combination of technologies they had experienced. Such identification is critical in light of the evolving nature of many distance education programs and the large number of changes they continue to experience. In addition, if the intent is to track developmental changes in the same participants through time, it is important to include participants' identification information in the satisfaction measures they complete. Tracking such information makes feasible a comparison of the satisfaction level of those who drop out with that of those who participate to completion.

How should such data be collected? Probably the single most widely used method of gathering learner satisfaction data is the written survey because it provides the most information for the cost and effort required. A survey can be administered by postal service, telephone, the Internet, or e-mail. Mail surveys allow the respondents to remain anonymous, respond freely and openly, and formulate answers carefully by reflecting on experiences with different phases of the program. Although telephone surveys offer the opportunity for the interviewer to follow up on the points made by respondents, they are more expensive and do not permit anonymity. Surveys administered by e-mail (with loss of respondent anonymity) or Internet provide excellent options when the participants have access to personal computers. However the survey is administered, the following suggestions may be helpful with regard to its content and format. The content refers to the subject matter to be included, whereas the format pertains to the structure and appearance—how the items are worded, their appearance on the page or the monitor, and the format used for answering the questions.

Content. Include questions regarding specific aspects of the course or the program under review. Seek suggestions from potential users of survey data during the design stage—this increases the likelihood of its use after the study is completed. Examine surveys used previously to collect the needed information; considerable time and effort can be saved. Include some of the old questions when new questions are added to focus on recent changes in the program. Make the questionnaire as short as possible—it is more likely to be completed by the intended audience.

Format. Use both fixed-alternative and open-ended questions. Fixed-alternative questions may include multiple-choice, true-false, and ratings matrix questions in which items (e.g., "the program is well designed") and the answers (e.g., "strongly agree, agree, undecided, disagree, strongly disagree") are presented in the form of a matrix. Open-ended but directed questions tend to be more helpful than simply asking for comments. Example: "Name one thing you *liked* and one thing you *did not like* about the program." Although helpful information for program improvement can be obtained from items that elicit specific comments, use a limited number of such items. To reduce ambiguity in the survey, pretest the questionnaire with a group of learners, and ask them to comment on the wording and clarity of questions. Potential respondents should receive a statement explaining that the information sought is being collected to examine the program and is not about them personally. Further, respondents should be given assurances that their responses are confidential and requested solely for analytical data collection—not for marketing or selling lists of personal data such as names, addresses, and phone numbers.

As we have emphasized throughout the chapter, employing multiple measures from multiple information sources is one of the core characteristics of valid and useful evaluations. When choosing measures to assess the selected variables (examples: achievement, attitudes, attrition, completion rate, and satisfaction), evaluate the specific approaches being considered by reflecting on the qualities of good measurement instruments. Is something important being assessed? Are we asking the right questions? Is the approach sensitive enough to detect small changes? Does the measure seem valid, reliable, and cost-effective? How will the data analysis be conducted? Who will use the findings? Why? In other words, outcome evaluation needs careful planning.

Data analysis always involves making some comparison, regardless of the nature the data collected to assess program effectiveness. Numbers in isolation, without a frame of reference or basis of comparison, seldom make much sense. Accordingly, evaluation designers should work with the end users of the evaluation in selecting the comparisons that will be significant in enhancing shared understanding, making judgments regarding instructional effectiveness, and strengthening both content and its mode of delivery. What are some possible bases for making useful comparisons? The outcomes of a distance learning program can be compared with the following:

- The outcomes of selected similar programs offered on campus

- The outcomes of selected similar distance education programs using different delivery modes

- The outcomes of similar programs offered via distance learning modes by another institution

- The outcomes of the same program offered the previous year (or in the previous cycle)

- The stated goals of the program

- Standards of minimum acceptability (e.g., basic licensing or accreditation standards)

- Faculty and administrators' expectations of program outcomes

This is not intended to be a comprehensive list of all available options. We do intend to emphasize that various possibilities should be discussed with potential users before designing the evaluation. Furthermore, a combination of these comparisons can give a full and balanced view of what is happening in the program (Patton, 1997).

The experience of attending a college or a university includes the social milieu of the campus, the informal interactions that take place outside the classes, and participation in cocurricular activities as well as the courses taken by a given student. Thus, the education of an individual is the integrated outcome of all experiences he or she has had during the college years. In conducting an evaluation of an entire program offered with different delivery modes (on-campus, Web-based, ITV, or combinations thereof), attention needs to be given not only to the outcomes of individual courses but also to the integrated outcome of the entire experience.

After making the relevant comparisons, the evaluation process moves on to the interpretation stage (Why the difference?) and judgments (Are such differences good or bad? Are they acceptable?). Data interpretation is a human process, not easily automated, as is the analysis of statistical data. Interpreting outcome data requires a good understanding of the program input and its processes. Engaging different users of evaluation brings varying perspectives to the task of interpreting and giving meaning to the data. Making judgments about the program follows analysis and interpretations. If external evaluators are involved in the process, their task is to facilitate the discussions on data interpretation and to help explore its various implications.

Whether evaluation is conducted in-house, externally, or as a combination of the two, it is essential to distinguish between analysis, interpretation, judgment, and recommendations. Insofar as possible, any recommendations should include a consideration of the benefits and costs of making the suggested changes, including the costs and risks of not making them (Patton, 1997). We now turn our attention to a discussion of costs and benefits.

Analysis of Costs and Outcomes

So far, our discussion of program evaluation has focused on input, processes, and outcomes. Although it is essential to document the extent to which the program has achieved the intended outcomes, it is just as critical to assess the costs of attempting to achieve those outcomes. Whether it is done impressionistically or through formal procedures, comparison of costs and outcomes is one of the most important considerations in deciding whether to expand, continue, or terminate a given program (Rossi, Freeman, & Lipsey, 1999).

One of the more confusing aspects of incorporating cost analysis into evaluation and decision making is that a number of different but related concepts and terms are often used interchangeably. Among these are *cost-benefit analysis* and *cost-effectiveness analysis*. The key difference between the two is the way in which the effects of a program are expressed in monetary terms. A cost-benefit analysis allows the evaluator to report the net benefits by subtracting the costs from the benefits. In contrast, cost-effectiveness analysis does not require that benefits be expressed in monetary terms. Instead, the effectiveness of a program in reaching the intended goals is related to what it costs to offer the program (Levin, 1983). In other words, different modes of delivering the same program or course are evaluated, and their costs compared. Thus, one can compare two or more delivery modes for helping students achieve the same outcomes. Given the large body of literature regarding the "no significant difference" among different modes of delivery (e.g., Russell, 1999), one possible approach may be to compare the costs of various modes of offering the same course. One may question, however, the assumption regarding the similarity of outcomes across delivery modes. This argument is especially relevant when the entire program is offered via distance learning. In light of these varying assumptions, the discussion in this section focuses on principles and concepts rather than prescribing a certain approach to relating costs to outcomes.

Cost Framework

When estimating the costs of offering a course or a program, a common practice is to consider both direct and indirect costs. Because indirect costs (or overhead) tend to be similar for courses provided by the same institution, we focus on the direct costs associated with the instructional modes included in making the comparison. Jewett and Davis (1999) suggest that at least five components are included in direct costs. Four of them are related to the course itself, and the other depends on the number of students enrolled in the course. A brief description of these components follows.

1. *Course development and design costs.* These costs relate to the human resources required to determine the course content, the learning outcomes, instructional strategies, and assessment techniques. These costs are incurred at least a semester or two before a distance learning course is actually offered. In addition, faculty developing such courses often need training or consultations related to teaching students at a distance. Costs associated with these activities also need to be included.

2. *Course production costs.* This category includes the expenses incurred in producing course materials, such as videotaped presentations, materials placed on the course Web site, syllabi, study guides, assessment measures, and assignments.

3. *Course maintenance costs.* These costs apply especially to courses that are produced for multiple distributions for several years. Because textbooks continue to be revised, resources needed to keep the course content current by regular updating must be budgeted. Failure to recognize maintenance costs may lead to the discontinuation of the course as its content becomes outdated.

4. *Course distribution costs.* If the course is being offered via ITV, it is necessary to budget for technical personnel at several sites, broadcasting costs, number of hours materials are being transmitted, royalty payments for copyrighted materials, and any studio charges or membership dues paid to maintain the broadcasting site. Course distribution costs also include expenses incurred in delivering printed materials, floppy disks, CD-ROMs, videotapes, and audiotapes to students.

5. *Support costs.* These costs include faculty and staff time related to interactions with individual students regarding the course content, moni-

toring of their participation, evaluation, and grade assignment. For online courses, faculty time devoted to communication with students can be considerable. If students are provided access to faculty by toll-free telephone, these expenses will depend on the number of students enrolled in the course and should be included in the support costs as well.

Relating Costs to Program Effectiveness

In evaluating different delivery methods, one approach is to assume that their outcomes are similar (Russell, 1999). Then, all components of the direct costs are determined and compared across modalities. Variable costs depend on the number of students enrolled in each mode of delivery. The fixed costs of the program are associated with the development of instructional materials, course production and distribution, and assessment procedures. The fixed costs may make distance education more expensive per student than on-campus classroom instruction when the number of students is rather small. It is possible, however, that after a certain level of enrollment is reached, the cost differences between distance and on-campus instruction may not be significant or may even make the distance instruction less expensive. Cost savings can be realized by creative networking that leads to course or program sharing among different colleges or universities. This strategy may significantly increase enrollment in the distance course and help distribute the course development costs across a larger number of students, thereby reducing the cost per student for the program. A cost simulation model developed by Jewett and Davis (1999) is now available to examine the cost efficiency of offering distance courses in collaboration with other institutions.

When the delivery methods under review may *not* be assumed to be similar with regard to the extent to which they achieve the expected outcomes, it is essential to examine their effectiveness in relation to the monetary costs. Cost-effectiveness analysis allows comparison and rank ordering of delivery modes by their per unit costs for reaching different outcomes. For example, in comparing distance instruction with in-class instruction for outcomes such as drop-out rate, learning outcomes, and graduation rates, cost-effectiveness ratios (costs/outcome) may be computed without having to assign a dollar value to the outcomes. Computing cost-effectiveness ratios for expected outcomes may be valuable in making comparisons through a number of years. When benefits can be expressed in monetary terms (e.g., tuition revenues), program efficiency can be judged by comparing costs to benefits. Because this is usually not the case in evaluation of distance programs, cost-effectiveness analysis remains the preferred approach.

An institution may choose to offer distance education even when it finds that such an approach is not cost-efficient. This decision must be based on the institutional mission of meeting the educational needs of place-bound students from a wide geographical area rather than serving only those who can participate in campus-based programs. In other words, a dollars-and-cents analysis alone cannot answer the question, "Should we offer this program?" Other factors such as institutional mission and value considerations play an important role in the process of making program-related decisions.

Conclusion

Although evaluation provides necessary information for possible improvements and decision making, quality teaching and learning must not be impaired by the excessive demands of conducting a comprehensive evaluation. Some distance education programs have progressed to the point of conducting comprehensive evaluations (Freddolino & Sutherland, 2000; Haga & Heitkamp, 2000; Potts & Hagen, 2000). Our experience indicates that it is better to undertake a series of smaller studies based on a variety of approaches using available data than to commit all available resources to a large-scale study employing a single approach that demands extensive data collection. Although it is customary to recommend one significantly rigorous plan, evaluation takes many forms in actual practice, and less rigorous approaches may be sufficient. Furthermore, it is wise not to declare allegiance to either a quantitative-scientific-summative methodology or a qualitative-naturalistic-descriptive methodology. Merit lies not in the form of inquiry but in the relevance the information has in answering questions that evaluation was designed to address.

Summary Tips

- Conduct an evaluation to make needed adjustments and modifications and to decide whether to expand, continue, or terminate the program.

- Engage potential users in all stages of the evaluation process.

- Focus on program inputs, learning processes, and student outcomes; this approach leads to a better understanding of why certain outcomes are not being achieved and helps in making needed improvements.

- Use application forms and essays to develop a profile of learner characteristics when appropriate.

- Use information from application essays to serve as a baseline for evaluating students' progress.

- Clearly identify key characteristics of alternatives to be compared; this information will be helpful in conceptualizing what distinguishes them from each other and why they differ or do not differ in their effectiveness.

- Examine how the program operates by observing what the learners actually do, how often they interact with each other, and what support services they use.

- Provide evidence of contact and quality of contact between faculty and students.

- Assess program effectiveness by collecting data on outcomes such as student learning (knowledge, skills, and attitudes and values), retention, and satisfaction for each delivery mode.

- Conduct data analysis separately for each outcome as well as for integrated outcomes.

- Be clear about definitions; uncertainty about what is actually being measured can lead to misinterpretations.

- Devote adequate attention to assessing the outcomes of the program as a whole in addition to evaluating the outcomes of individual courses.

- Collect evaluation data on input, processes, and outcomes by using multiple measures.

- Use existing data, whenever possible.

- Obtain needed information from multiple sources (e.g., students, faculty, administrators, alumni, and employers).

- Interpret evaluation data by comparing alternatives expected to achieve the same outcomes.

- Relate program outcomes to costs by conducting cost-effectiveness analysis for all alternatives that are being compared.

- Report the evaluation findings to faculty members promptly to help them improve teaching effectiveness.

$\mathbf{WWW} \longrightarrow$ At our Sage Web site, www.sagepub.com/mehrotra

---

On our companion Web site, we present examples of outcomes evaluations in one of our own distance education courses, a follow-up study of graduates of a master of education program offered via distance learning, and evaluation questionnaires. Also included is information about books and journals related to evaluation of distance programs.

References

Astin, A. W. (1991). *Assessment for excellence: The philosophy and practice of assessment and evaluation in higher education.* New York: Macmillan.

Freddolino, P., & Sutherland, C. (2000). Assessing the comparability of classroom environments in graduate social work education delivered via interactive television. *Journal of Social Work Education, 36*(1), 115-129.

Haga, M., & Heitkamp, T. (2000). Bringing social work education to the prairie. *Journal of Social Work Education, 36*(2), 309-324.

Jewett, F., & Davis, D. (1999). *Cost simulation model (bridge).* Retrieved April 12, 2001, from the World Wide Web: www.calstate.edu/special_projects/mediated_instr/Bridge/index.html

Levin, H. M. (1983). *Cost effectiveness: A primer.* Beverly Hills, CA: Sage.

Mehrotra, C. M. (1999, April). Using assessment to strengthen distance learning programs. In S. E. Van Kollenburg (Ed.), *A collection of papers on self-study and institutional improvement* (pp. 64-67). Chicago: North Central

Association of Colleges and Schools, Commission on Institutions of Higher Education.

Merisotis, J. P. (1999, September-October). The "what is the difference" debate. *Academe, 85*(5), 47-51.

Patton, M. Q. (1997). *Utilization-focused evaluation.* Thousand Oaks, CA: Sage.

Potts, M., & Hagan, C. (2000). Going the distance: Using systems theory to design, implement, and evaluate a distance education program. *Journal of Social Work Education, 36*(1), 131-145.

Powell, R., Conway, C., & Ross, L. (1990). Effects of student predisposing characteristics on student success. *Journal of Distance Education, 5*(1), 20-37.

Rossi, P. H., Freeman, H. E., & Lipsey, M. W. (1999). *Evaluation: A systematic approach* (6th ed.). Thousand Oaks, CA: Sage.

Russell, T. L. (1999). *The "no significant difference" phenomenon as reported in 355 research reports, summaries and papers.* Raleigh: North Carolina State University Office of Instructional Telecommunications.

11

Accreditation

Most colleges and universities in the United States are accredited by one of the country's eight regional accrediting commissions. In addition, specific programs within these institutions are accredited by national professional associations such as those for engineering, medicine, law, business, education, psychology, and social work. Both institutional accreditation and specialized accreditation are voluntary and have two fundamental purposes: quality assurance and institutional/ program improvement. Accrediting bodies evaluate more than formal educational activities; they also assess such characteristics as governance and administration, financial stability, admissions and student personnel services, institutional resources, student academic achievement, institutional effectiveness, and relationships with constituencies outside the institution. In other words, as we discussed in Chapter 10, evaluators focus on inputs, processes, and outcomes for the institution as a whole.

Although the eight regional accrediting commissions are independent of one another, they cooperate extensively and recognize one another's accreditation. In addition, they take cognizance of the standards set by professional bodies and require the affiliated institutions to keep them abreast of significant changes in their accreditation status with specialized agencies. This cooperation between accrediting agencies furthers the standards that promote educational quality and allows the institutions to explore new ways of achieving their stated goals and objectives. Because new information technologies are accelerating the globalization of higher education, it is essential to extend such cooperation and exchange of ideas and information to the international level as well.

The quality of educational experience that students receive in distance learning programs has been the subject of both criticism and debate from the public, legislators, and educators themselves. Therefore, it is not surprising that almost all accrediting agencies now require higher education institutions to address such questions as these:

- How can the institution ensure the quality of distance learning courses and programs?

- What safeguards can the institution employ to sustain program integrity and deter potential abuses?

- How can this nontraditional delivery system help an institution realize its stated goals and objectives?

The guidelines developed by accrediting agencies can help the institutions respond to some of the internal and external queries concerning quality assurance as they contemplate the establishment, expansion, or enhancement of distance learning programs. In the following section, we provide the guidelines for distance learning programs that are currently used by all the regional accrediting associations. These guidelines are based on an extension of the principles developed by the Western Interstate Commission on Higher Education (WICHE).

Guidelines for Distance Learning

The following guidelines were approved by the Commission on Institutions of Higher Education, North Central Association of Colleges and Schools (NCA) in March 1997. The commission considers such statements to be working documents, subject to revision, and continues to review their usefulness as more is learned from institutions engaged in exploring new modes of delivery from educational teams and from the broader higher education community and the public. Although these guidelines represent a working document under constant review, they provide a framework to readers contemplating developing distance learning programs.

Curriculum and Instruction

Programs provide for timely and appropriate interaction between students and faculty, and among students.

The institution's faculty assumes responsibility for and exercises oversight over distance education, ensuring both the rigor of programs and the quality of instruction.

The institution ensures that the technology used is appropriate to the nature and objectives of the programs.

The institution ensures the currency of materials, programs, and courses.

The institution's distance education policies are clear concerning ownership of materials, faculty compensation, copyright issues, and the utilization of revenue derived from the creation and production of software, telecourses, or other media products.

The institution provides appropriate faculty support services specifically related to distance education.

The institution provides appropriate training for faculty who teach in distance education programs.

Evaluation and Assessment

The institution assesses student capability to succeed in distance education programs and applies this information to admission and recruiting policies and decisions.

The institution evaluates the educational effectiveness of its distance education programs (including assessments of student learning outcomes, student retention, and student satisfaction) to ensure comparability to campus-based programs.

The institution ensures the integrity of student work and the credibility of the degrees and credits it awards.

Library and Learning Resources

The institution ensures that students have access to and can effectively use appropriate library resources.

The institution monitors whether students make appropriate use of learning resources.

The institution provides laboratories, facilities, and equipment appropriate to the courses or programs.

Student Services

The institution provides adequate access to the range of student services appropriate to support the programs, including admissions, financial aid, academic advising, delivery of course materials, and placement and counseling.

The institution provides an adequate means for resolving student complaints.

The institution provides students advertising, recruiting, and admissions information that adequately and accurately represents the programs, requirements, and services available.

The institution ensures that students admitted possess the knowledge and equipment necessary to use the technology employed in the program, and provides aid to students who are experiencing difficulty using the required technology.

Facilities and Finances

The institution possesses the equipment and technical expertise required for distance education.

The institution's long range planning, budgeting, and policy development processes reflect the facilities, staffing, equipment and other resources essential to the viability and effectiveness of the distance learning program. (pp. 171-172)

Providing Evidence Regarding the Program's Effectiveness in Meeting the Guidelines

All accrediting agencies include two components in conducting comprehensive evaluations: institutional self-study and peer evaluation. It is expected that the institution seeking accreditation plans and undertakes a self-study process to determine how well it meets the stated requirements and criteria and to clarify its plans for improving and enhancing its programs and operations. The findings of this self-study are presented in a report that constitutes the institution's application for accreditation and also serves as the basis for an evaluation site visit by peers from accredited institutions.

The self-study report and the evaluation process include all aspects of the institution and its programs. Our discussion in this chapter, however, focuses mainly on how distance learning programs meet the accreditation guidelines. This documentation is included in the self-study report that the institution submits to the accrediting agency.

Curriculum and Instruction

A. *Programs provide for timely and appropriate interaction between students and faculty and among students.*

This requirement is based on the premise that the more interactive the instruction, the more effective the learning outcome is likely to be (Sumler & Zirkin, 1995). In Chapter 3, we suggested a variety of strategies to encourage faculty-student contact and to promote reciprocity and cooperation among students. While preparing the self-study report, the institution should review these strategies and determine which of them will be (or are being) used in each of the distance courses. The reviewers would be interested in learning the extent to which these strategies have been used, what has worked well, and what not so well. They would also like to know how using these strategies affects the instructors' workloads, the maximum class size for the courses, and the number of courses the instructors teach in a given term. In short, this section of the self-study should include specific evidence of substantial interactivity among students and between students and faculty.

For example, for an online course, logs could be submitted of chat room activity, e-mails to the instructors, and use of the toll-free telephone number. For an ITV course, the institution could make available videotapes of in-class, cross-site, and within-site student-student and student-instructor discussions. Data from end-of-course evaluations regarding students' assessments of the amount and quality of interaction and connectivity in the course could also be included.

B. *The institution's faculty assumes responsibility for and exercises oversight of distance education, ensuring both the rigor of programs and the quality of instruction.*

The accrediting bodies expect the institutions to document that faculty members control the creation of course content and maintain oversight of the implementation of all distance programs. We offer the following suggestions to address these requirements:

- Provide documentation that the program or the institution's curriculum committee is responsible for curriculum development and evaluation. Indicate if the faculty who designed distance courses are the same individuals who teach these courses in the on-campus program. If the same faculty are not responsible for the two modes of delivery, include evidence of how the two sets of instructors work together to ensure equivalence in the two offerings.

- Provide evidence how the syllabi for the distance courses are designed to achieve the same learning outcomes as the companion on-campus courses.

- If the program employs part-time faculty, include evidence demonstrating how they are selected, how they interact with core faculty, and what methods are used to ensure that they maintain standards similar to those used for on-campus courses.

C. *The institution ensures that the technology used is appropriate to the nature and objectives of the programs.*

This requirement may be addressed by describing the technology or combination of technologies used for delivering the program, indicating why these technologies were selected, and explaining how they match the program goals and objectives. The discussion should detail how the program outcomes were clarified initially and then how the technology was selected to best fulfill the desired program functions and outcomes.

This part of the self-study report should include documentation demonstrating that students have both access to the technologies used in the program and the knowledge and skills necessary to use them. In Chapter 3, we suggested that instruction be made available to students who need to learn how to use technology effectively to access learning resources. If the program design includes a module on using technology or requires that students have access to specific technologies and know how to use them, the self-study report should include a discussion of these requirements and how they are met. The report should also describe the specific steps taken by the institution to ensure that those traditionally underrepresented in higher education (e.g., African Americans, Hispanics, and Native Americans, and those from lower income levels) are not at a distinct disadvantage in having increased access to distance courses. Furthermore, this discussion should also include how the program addresses the needs of students with various disabilities.

D. *The institution ensures the currency of materials, programs, and courses.*

Accrediting bodies will look for documentation that the mechanisms have been created to ensure the currency of materials, programs, and courses. The report should include a discussion of who is responsible for monitoring the program content, its delivery methods, and the faculty preparation and a description of the external and internal indicators that provide evidence for currency of all aspects of the distance program. Here are some possible approaches that may be used to address this requirement:

- Describe the composition of the faculty committee responsible for conducting program reviews, and explain the cycle that the committee uses to select the programs reviewed in a given year.

- Include a copy of the checklist used by the program director and during the review process.

- Include a description of how the committee obtains input from an external reviewer, if applicable.

- Analyze the syllabi for the past 5 years to determine what changes have been made and how they reflect the advances in the field.

- Examine data from sources such as employer surveys, alumni surveys, licensing examinations, and graduate record examinations.

- Describe how the assessment findings are used to make programmatic improvements on a regular basis.

- Outline the support that the institution provides faculty to incorporate new advances in their courses.

As we stated in Chapter 10, having such information readily available is useful not only for accreditation purposes but also for program marketing and institutional advancement. In addition, employers of program graduates also appreciate knowing that the institution makes continual efforts to keep its programs current. This in turn facilitates the placement of graduates.

E. *The institution's distance education policies are clear concerning (a) ownership of materials; (b) faculty compensation; (c) copyright issues; and (d) use of revenues derived from the creation and production of software, telecourses, or other media products.*

The self-study report should refer the readers to the institution's faculty handbook describing the policies that have been approved regarding the ownership of the distance learning materials, copyright issues, and use of revenues. The American Association of University Professors (AAUP, 2000) Special Committee on Distance Education and Intellectual Property Issues suggested that copyright of materials produced by the faculty members should belong to them except when they have been produced for a specific requirement of employment or as an assigned institutional duty. In addition, a distance learning course may be co-owned by an institution and a faculty member when he or she contributes the courseware and the institution provides specialized service such as technical support to adapt the courseware for use in a distance learning environment. Interested readers may consult the

AAUP's distance education policies at its Web site (www.aaup.org/ DistncEd.htm). The key point is that accrediting bodies want to ensure that the institution has thought through its policies with regard to the ownership of distance education courses and materials, has obtained approval of the policies by the board of trustees, and has included them in the faculty handbook. Taking these steps promotes a clear understanding by the faculty before they design distance education materials.

F. *The institution provides appropriate faculty support services specifically related to distance education.*

This requirement is included to ensure that an integrated team remains available to support faculty efforts related to distance education. Who are the members of this team? Although there may be some variability across institutions, examples of team members include technology support staff, media specialists, counselors, library service personnel, distribution clerks, and site administrators. Each member of the team contributes in unique ways toward the goal of providing uninterrupted services essential for teaching and learning. Without such support, distance learning programs cannot continue to operate effectively and efficiently.

Because the smooth functioning of programs demands critical faculty support services, self-study reports must provide a detailed description of the arrangements that have been made in each of the areas outlined above. In addition, it is important to track student use of various services (e.g., library, financial aid, registrar, counseling, and placement) and to include such records in the self-study report. Although technology makes it easier to accomplish the tracking with minimum additional work, it is important to design a systematic plan ahead of time and maintain the needed records for purposes of accreditation and program improvement.

G. *The institution provides appropriate training for faculty who teach in distance education programs.*

In this section of the self-study report, the institution is expected to describe how faculty members are selected, how they are assisted in making the transition from classroom teaching to distance instruction and how they are assessed in this process, what technical assistance in course development is made available to them and how they are encouraged to use it, what training instructors receive throughout the progression of the program, and what written resources are provided to assist them in dealing with student-related issues arising in distance programs.

The institution needs to document how it offers faculty training, peer mentoring, and individualized consultation and support on a continuing basis, rather than only when a program is being launched. In addition to describing the training activities and resources, the report should include a profile of the participating faculty, explain how faculty have used the available training and support, and document how the support has contributed to the faculty members' professional development and the ways that it has affected their teaching in campus-based courses. Thus, the report should include not only a description of the training activities but their evaluation as well.

Evaluation and Assessment

A. *The institution assesses student capability to succeed in distance education programs and applies this information to admission and recruiting policies and decisions.*

In Chapter 10, we saw that evaluation of distance programs focuses not only on outcomes but on input and processes as well. The first requirement in the accreditation guidelines concerns the policies and procedures that a given institution has in place with regard to admission of students to the program. The self-study report should address this requirement by outlining the admission criteria that faculty have established to ensure that accepted students have the abilities, preparation, and motivation essential for success in a distance learning program (see Chapter 10 for examples of procedures used to obtain information with regard to the admission requirements). These requirements for success in a distance format are in addition to the program-specific standards that faculty have established for all modes of delivery. Some accrediting bodies want to be assured that the same standards are used for both distance and campus-based offerings of the program.

Simply outlining admission criteria is insufficient. Accrediting agencies also expect the institution to describe who is responsible for implementing the admission procedures, monitoring the process, and using the findings to make modifications and adjustments as necessary. This discussion should include summary tables with information on applicant characteristics regarding the stated criteria. The table entries should distinguish between those who were accepted and those who were denied admission, as well as indicating students who were provisionally accepted. A concluding section should present the highlights of what has been learned as a result of monitoring the process of attracting a critical mass of students, reviewing their application materials, making admission decisions, and tracking their progress. Reflecting on this process will help the institution identify the characteristics of students who successfully complete the distance learning program. This information is helpful in fine-tuning the admission criteria, the methods for obtaining the needed information from the applicants, and the procedures for making the selection decisions.

B. *The institution evaluates the educational effectiveness of its distance education programs (including assessment of student learning outcomes, student retention, and student satisfaction) to ensure comparability with campus-based programs.*

This section of the self-study report focuses on providing evidence regarding the effectiveness of the program in achieving the expected outcomes. Chapter 10 offers a detailed discussion of methods for assessing program effectiveness. All self-study reports include a comprehensive analysis of the institutionwide assessment plan, its implementation, and its findings as a means of documenting the measurement of student learning outcomes. It follows that the criteria for assessing distance education programs should be consistent with those used by the institution as a whole and should be used to compare the relative effectiveness of alternate modes of institutional delivery.

In light of the concern about the drop-out rate in distance programs, this section of the self-study report should describe the procedures adopted to track student progress in the program. Findings regarding retention rate should be presented and compared with campus-based programs in the same discipline. If the data on student satisfaction are also reported for various modes of program delivery, reviewers will appreciate having access to copies of the survey instruments used to collect data. In our experience, it is a good idea to include student and alumni satisfaction data for a number of years. This allows the reviewers to assess the progress that the program has made by implementing important changes based on student input.

C. The institution ensures the integrity of student work and the credibility of the degrees it awards.

The self-study report should document that the students in distance programs receive the quality of education comparable with what on-site students receive. In Chapters 9 and 10, we suggested strategies for ensuring the integrity of student work and the credibility of degrees that are awarded. Examples of these strategies include developing learning contracts with students that allow them to achieve the course outcomes; having tests proctored by locally assigned individuals; holding unannounced telephone discussions between the instructor and the students; and having students defend their thesis (or report of their research) in the traditional manner before a faculty committee, although the discussion may take place via ITV or speakerphone. Although this is not a comprehensive list of strategies, those items reviewed here emphasize the importance of creating innovative ways to ensure the integrity of student work and presenting those methods in the self-study report.

If the distance education program is offered in a professional area (such as nursing, physical therapy, and health information administration) in which program graduates take a licensing exam as a prerequisite to employment, the institution should monitor student performance on these exams and present an analysis of the data as an indication of the credibility of the degrees it awards in these disciplines. The performance of program graduates on licensing exams offers evidence useful in assessing and documenting program outcomes at no additional cost to the program because such external measures provide comparisons with national, regional, or state statistics.

Accrediting agencies expect institutions to show that they have procedures in place to monitor the integrity of student work and that these procedures are used continually. In addition, institutions are expected to document the comparability of alternative modes of delivering the same program. Because the diplomas that students receive are the same no matter what delivery mode is used, the learning outcomes must be the same as well.

Library and Learning Resources

A. *The institution ensures that students have access to and can effectively use appropriate library resources.*

Many students enrolled in distance programs experience a sense of isolation and concern about the equivalence of their learning experiences to traditional on-campus instruction. One important way to ensure equivalence of the learning experiences is to provide appropriate library resources that are accessible to and usable by *all* students. Self-study reports should explain how the students are provided with hands-on training and information to aid them in securing materials through electronic databases, interlibrary loans, electronic reserves, government archives, news services, and so on. With the rapid pace at which traditional libraries are being complemented (or supplanted?) by computer networks and online retrieval systems, accrediting bodies expect that institutions will substantiate that students and faculty are provided with orientation and training sessions to access information in new ways. Evidence regarding the currency and effectiveness of these sessions needs to be included.

Making library resources and information services available is not enough. An easily accessible support system that assists learners in making effective use of these resources throughout the program must be created and documented. Accrediting agencies expect that distance education programs will provide information such as this: What library resources have been made available to students enrolled in the program? How do the students receive the information training and orientation that they need to make effective use of new information technologies? What support systems are in place to provide them with assistance that they may need to access the information? How does the institution ensure their effectiveness? What system is in place to address student complaints about these resources?

B. *The institution monitors whether students make appropriate use of learning resources.*

Students must use a full range of learning resources (textbooks, journal articles, monographs, project reports, Internet links, group work, etc.) to achieve the professed program outcomes. The grades that students receive in the course reflect their performance on tests, assignments, presentations, participation in discussion groups, group assignments, and demonstrations. In view of the variety of learning resources required to achieve the outcomes related to knowledge, attitudes and values, skills, and behaviors, the institution needs to monitor and document that students are making appropriate use of the wide range of learning resources. The underlying rationale for this requirement is that learning how to learn is as important as achieving the course outcomes. The guidelines are based on the premise that simply making learning resources available does not guarantee that all students are using them effectively to attain the expected outcomes.

In summary, the self-study report should include the following:

1. A description of the procedures used to monitor student use of the learning resources

2. An analysis of data collected by the monitoring process

3. A discussion of how the findings are used for enhancement of support services

C. *The institution provides laboratories, facilities, and equipment appropriate to the courses or programs.*

The accrediting agencies want assurance that the students have access to laboratories, clinical facilities, fieldwork sites, and equipment essential to achieving program goals. Such evidence is critical in demonstrating that the learning experiences of students in distance programs are equivalent to those enrolled in campus-based programs. If, for example, a counseling psychology program is offered by distance learning, how do the students receive practical training in various aspects of the counseling process? How do they receive supervision and feedback? How do they demonstrate that they have developed the required skills and competencies? If the institution has developed partnerships with providers of counseling services in different communities, it should include copies of these agreements in the self-study report submitted to the accreditation agency. In other words, it is expected that all distance programs include documentation regarding the arrangements they have made to provide students with easy access to the laboratories, facilities, and equipment needed for various components of the program. Information also should be included regarding students' experience with these resources, modifications, and adjustments that have been made through time and plans for the future.

Student Services

In reviewing distance learning programs, all accrediting agencies conduct a rigorous assessment of the quality of student services. Although on the surface, such an emphasis may reflect continuing concern about the low rates of course program completion and the large number of student complaints regarding some programs, the underlying rationale has to do with the critical role played by student support in the effectiveness of distance education programs. Phipps, Wellman, and Merisotis (1998) observed that a focus on adequate student support as an essential element of teaching and learning may be one of the most distinctive indicators of the quality of distance learning environments. The following subsections outline approaches that may be used to document the quality of student services.

A. *The institution provides adequate access to the range of student services appropriate to support the programs, including admissions, financial aid, academic advising, delivery of course materials, and placement and counseling.*

The self-study report should include a detailed discussion regarding the four categories of student services listed above. In the section on evaluation and assessment, we noted that the institution should outline the criteria that it uses to accept students into the program and should substantiate that those criteria are equivalent to those used in the campus-based program. Because a large number of nontraditional students enroll in distance programs, answers to the following questions should be readily available:

- Does the institution give credit for what students have learned on the job or through other life experiences? How is the prior learning assessed and documented? What fees, if any, are charged for this service?

- Does the institution allow students to "test out" of a course or courses? If so, are standardized exams used, such as College Level Examination Program exams developed by the Educational Testing Service?

- Can a student take courses offered by a program before being admitted to a program?

- Will the institution accept transfer credits in the program? If yes, how many?

The accrediting agencies like to know institutional policies regarding the above questions, how those policies are communicated to potential participants, how they are implemented, and how the institution monitors their impact on program outcomes. The site visitors are especially interested in learning how the institution ensures the equivalence of transfer credits to courses offered in its on-campus program. For example, consider the implications of an institutional policy that allows students to complete all the general education requirements before applying for admission to a professional program offered by distance learning. In this scenario, the institution is expected to document that the transfer students have acquired the expected knowledge, skills, and attitudes and values at another institution judged necessary for success in the professional program.

In addition to explaining the policies and procedures related to admissions, the self-study report should include information regarding tuition, fees, and financial aid for the program. Simply listing amounts for each of these categories is not adequate. The report should describe how this information is made available to distance learners, the effectiveness of the staff members in answering students' questions, and the level of students' satisfaction with the service they receive from the institution. Given the continuing changes in the financial aid regulations, the institution should report how it keeps itself abreast of new developments and how it incorporates up-to-date information in the materials that it prepares for potential participants.

One of the major frustrations of distance learners is the difficulty that they experience in contacting the appropriate person or office to answer their questions related to admissions, registration, and financial aid. It is a good idea to include a discussion in the self-study report highlighting how the institution has created a single contact for the students to obtain the information needed to enroll in the program.

Academic advising plays a critical role in helping students weave through the institutional requirements and processes. The self-study report should clearly explain how the advising process works in a distance learning environment, how many students are assigned to an academic adviser in a given term, what training programs have been offered to advisers new to working with students at a distance, what the institution has learned from evaluating the process of academic advising, and how the advising process has (one hopes) improved through time.

The self-study report also should detail how the course materials are delivered to the learners. This section includes a description of the information that students receive after they have been accepted in the program. For example, in a video-based course, students may receive (a) a course guide that offers specific information about the course, its outcomes and objectives, policies, and procedures; (b) videotaped presentations; (c) session notes; and (d) textbook(s). If the course is offered via the Internet, the students receive a course guide, textbook(s), and logon information. This section describes how the program ensures coordination between the admissions process, academic advising, registration, and delivery of course materials. Because lack of coordination may delay the delivery of course materials and create unnecessary anxiety among the students, the self-study report should describe what steps have been taken to achieve effective coordination between various offices and how satisfied the students are with the services they receive in this regard.

In addition to providing students with hands-on training and information on using the technology that the program employs to deliver course materials, the institution is also expected to make technical assistance available to all students throughout the duration of the program. The self-study report should describe what avenues (e.g., toll-free number, e-mail, and online tutorial) have been afforded to students, which members of the technical staff have been assigned these responsibilities, and how they work together to improve the technical support using student feedback. The site visitors appreciate reviewing the log that the program staff maintains regarding student requests for technical support and when and how they were handled. Evaluators need to know who provides technical support, when such support is available (hours per day, days per week), and the level of student satisfaction with the support.

Many adult students enroll in professional programs with the goal of seeking a job, changing jobs, or beginning a career. Accrediting agencies therefore assess what counseling services have been made available to distance learners, how frequently they have been used, and how satisfied the students are with these services. We suggest that the self-study report should include a description of these services (their content focus and delivery mode), data on their use by the students, evaluation by the students, and statistics regarding student placement.

B. The institution provides an adequate means for resolving student complaints.

The accrediting agencies need assurance that questions directed to all members of the program staff are answered accurately and quickly, with a structured system in place to address student complaints. They expect the self-study report to include a discussion of the system that the program has designed to respond to students' questions, to address student complaints, and to make students aware of the process and procedures that are in place to resolve their complaints. As we have noted earlier, it is important to maintain systematic records regarding the complaints received, what they dealt with, when and how they were addressed, and who was responsible for resolving them. Having access to these records allows the site visitors to randomly interview a small sample of students and assess their satisfaction with how their complaints were resolved. When a large number of complaints are in the same focus area (e.g., financial aid, technical support, or library services) during a given period, the accrediting bodies expect the program to document what steps it has taken to improve these services, what results it has achieved, and how it has designed mechanisms to prevent such problems in the future.

C. *The institution provides students with advertising, recruiting, and admission information that adequately and accurately represents the program, requirements, and services available.*

Potential participants in a distance education program may have limited familiarity with the program's content, requirements, delivery method, and available services. Thus, institutions are expected to explain what strategies (e.g., college bulletins, fact sheets, program brochures, Web sites, and information sessions) they use to make the essential information available to prospective learners, how they assess the effectiveness of different modalities, and how they use assessment findings to strengthen their efforts. The self-study report should include examples of recruitment materials that the program has used along with evidence regarding their effectiveness in reaching the intended audience and providing the needed information. We suggest including comparative data regarding the methods that the program has employed to attract various segments of the target population, including those from underrepresented groups.

The accrediting bodies also expect the institution to document that marketing materials accurately represent all aspects of the program in an easy-to-understand language and style. Presenting an accurate description of the program, its outcomes, and the demands it places on the participants increases the likelihood of attracting learners who have the potential to do well in the new format. The self-study report should clearly describe the procedures that were used in designing the materials, in field testing the drafts, and in securing internal approvals to offer the program.

D. *The institution ensures that students admitted possess the knowledge and the equipment necessary to use the technology employed in the program and provides aid to students who are experiencing difficulty using the required technology.*

The institution is expected to document how it ensures that the students admitted to the program possess the knowledge and equipment essential to participate in all aspects of the program. This should not be surprising because modern distance education programs often use sophisticated technology to deliver course content and maintain student-faculty interaction. If the institution evaluates applicants' ability to participate in Internet-based distance learning, it should include results of such assessment in the self-study. The university or college should explain in some detail how it addresses the needs of applicants who do not have the technology-related knowledge and skills. Furthermore, if the institution has designed a self-instructional program for underprepared participants, it should include a description of program content, its mode of delivery, and evidence regarding its effectiveness. Because these students often need continuing technical support, the self-study report should explain what resources were made available, how frequently they were used by the target audience, and to what extent they addressed critical needs.

Facilities and Finances

This section of the guidelines focuses on facilities and finances essential to designing a quality program, making it accessible to the intended audience, assessing it on a continuing basis, and keeping it up to date. The accrediting bodies expect to review evidence regarding institutional commitment to quality and effectiveness in all aspects of the learning environment.

A. *The institution possesses the equipment and technical expertise required for distance education.*

The self-study report should include a detailed description of (a) what equipment is available to offer the distance program; (b) what resources have been earmarked to upgrade essential equipment on a regular basis; (c) what technical expertise is available to assist the faculty in designing, implementing, and assessing the program; and (d) how the faculty and technical staff work together to ensure an effective and a coherent learning environment. Simply describing the equipment and technical expertise is not sufficient. It is essential to document that the program has the equipment needed to make the program accessible to the target audience and to help them achieve the expected outcomes. Similarly, the institution needs to substantiate that faculty members have continuing access to the technical expertise required to keep their program both effective and efficient. As noted earlier, the self-study must document that technical support is available to all students.

B. *The institution's long-range planning, budgeting, and policy development processes reflect the facilities, staffing, equipment, and other resources essential to the viability and effectiveness of the distance learning program.*

This element of the guidelines focuses on institutional context and commitment to distance education. Therefore, the self-study should include evidence demonstrating how distance programs both support and extend the institution's mission and how the requisite policies and resources are integrated into the policy framework of the institution as a whole. Financial and administrative commitment to building and maintaining the distance education infrastructure must be documented. A recent report (Institute for Higher Education Policy, 2000) suggests that this documentation should address the following:

1. How faculty are provided professional incentives to explore innovative course designs aimed at addressing the educational needs of a diverse student body

2. How the tenure, promotion, and other reward systems have been redesigned to recognize effective teaching of distance courses

3. What technology plan has been developed to help faculty ensure high academic standards

4. What security measures are in place to ensure integrity and validity of information

5. What technical support is available to students for each educational technology hardware, software, and delivery system required in the program

6. What articulation and transfer policies have been developed to accept courses taken by students at other institutions

7. How changes in technology are introduced to ensure maximum benefit to students and faculty

Most certainly, this is not a comprehensive list of all elements that need to be addressed to demonstrate that distance programs are integral to the institution's processes and operations. We have included these particular items to illustrate the nature of issues that faculty, administrators, and other members of the program team should keep in mind as they launch their distance learning programs, monitor their day-to-day functioning, and assess their effectiveness.

Conclusion

The guidelines that we have used to prepare this chapter were developed in March 1997 by the North Central Association, now called the Higher Learning Commission of the North Central Association of Colleges and Schools. Since that time, distance learning has rapidly become an increasingly important component of higher education. In addition to the growing number of colleges and universities, new nontraditional providers are offering distance courses and programs. This trend is likely to continue. Furthermore, the flexibility of distance instruction to serve national and international student populations has created the need for consistency in the principles and procedures used by the eight regional accrediting commissions in evaluating these activities. Given this need for ensuring cross-regional consistency, the eight commissions collectively, through the Council of Regional Accrediting Commissions, contracted with the Western Cooperative for Educational Telecommunication to develop a detailed elucidation of elements that exemplify quality in distance education. This detailed explanation has now become available in a document titled *Best Practices for Electronically Offered Degree and Certificate Programs* (Council of Regional Accrediting Commissions, 2001). The *Best Practices* document is now available at the Higher Learning Commission's Web site (www. ncahigherlearningcommission.org). All regional commissions are now using these practices along with their respective accreditation standards to ensure quality in distance instruction. The *Best Practices* are not new evaluative criteria, nor are they designed to serve as a checklist that the site visitors would use to review distance programs. Instead, these practices should be viewed as methods of formalizing how the well-established essentials of institutional quality outlined in regional accreditation standards are applicable to distance instruction. The availability of this elucidation of elements of quality should be helpful not only to the accrediting commissions across the country but to distance education providers as well.

The accrediting bodies consider this document subject to revision in light of what is learned in the process of using the available technologies and assessing their effectiveness in fostering student learning. Given the dramatic pace with which the new technologies continue to emerge, their instructional uses continue to be developed, and the evaluation issues continue to surface, it is clear that there will be a continuing need to reexamine and revise the *Best Practices* document. The key questions, however, will remain the same: What instructional methods can be used to help students achieve the intended learning outcomes effectively, and how can the achievement of these outcomes for individual students and for the program as a whole be documented?

Summary Tips

- Collect information in each of the focus areas systematically, and use technology to maintain the needed records: Preparation for accreditation is a continuing process.

- Follow the latest guidelines published by the accrediting agency, and present specific documentation for the components included in the guidelines.

- Document how the distance programs both support and extend the institution's role and mission.

- Explain how the work of other organizations is monitored and evaluated to ensure institutional integrity if important elements of a program are outsourced.

- Describe how students' characteristics are taken into account in designing and implementing the services that they need to achieve the learning outcomes, particularly after reflecting on the continuing increase in the diversity of the student population.

- Include evidence illustrating how the institution provides program faculty the support that they need in designing, implementing, and evaluating distance programs.

- Make other evidence (videotapes, logs of student interactions with each other and with the instructor, and financial records) not included in the self-study report available to evaluators during the on-site visit.

- Engage all members of the program team in the self-assessment process.

- Keep the campus community apprised of the progress of the self-study efforts and evaluators' comments during the site visit.

- Use the strategies outlined in Chapters 9 and 10 to substantiate how student learning is assessed, how program effectiveness is determined, and how the evaluation findings are used to guide program improvement. The self-study report should be evaluative, rather than descriptive.

- Provide a developmental picture showing how the program has continued to evolve in view of advances in the substantive areas, instructional methodology, and computer technology.

- Present assessment of distance programs in the context of the institutionwide evaluation of academic programs using the inputs, processes, and outcomes framework.

Although the previous tips provide general suggestions that may be helpful in preparing for an accreditation review, Tables 11.1 through 11.5 present examples of documentation that may be presented for each of the focus areas. These examples are not intended to be a comprehensive list of all possible ways of providing evidence regarding different review criteria. Instead, they should be viewed as a starting point from which to generate new approaches aimed at addressing the underlying intent of each criterion.

Www ▶ At our Sage Web site, www.sagepub.com/mehrotra

Visit our companion Web site to find links to electronic resources related to accreditation agencies and their guidelines, publications on preparation of a self-study report, concept papers on international perspectives regarding standards, and discussion of quality assurance issues in the changing field of distance education.

TABLE 11.1 Possible Documentation Methods for the Curriculum and Instruction Criteria

Review Focus	*Examples of Documentation*
Timely and appropriate interaction between students and faculty and among students	Sample logs of chat room activity, e-mails to instructors, use of toll-free telephone number; sample of video-tapes documenting discussions; students' assessment of interactions in the course
Faculty responsibility for and oversight of the course	Curriculum development and evaluation process; syllabi; relationship between faculty for on-campus and distance courses
Technology appropriate to the nature and objectives of the program	Technologies and their match to the course/program goals; students have access to technologies and have the knowledge and skills to use them
Currency of materials, programs, and courses	Mechanisms and indicators used to ensure currency; who is responsible for monitoring program content, delivery methods, and faculty preparation
Policies regarding ownership of materials, faculty compensation, copyright issues, and use of revenues	Faculty handbook; policies regarding use of revenues
Availability of faculty support services	Support provided by technology support staff, media specialists, counselors, library staff, distribution clerks, and site administrators
Training for faculty	Selection and training of faculty and its evaluation

TABLE 11.2 Possible Documentation Methods for the Evaluation and Assessment Criteria

Review Focus	Examples of Documentation
Assessment of students' capability for admitting them to the program	Admission criteria used to accept students in the program; summary tables with information on applicants' characteristics and decisions made in each case
Program evaluation	Assessment of student learning outcomes, student retention, and student satisfaction
Integrity of student work and the credibility of the degrees	Procedures used to monitor integrity of students' work; evidence regarding the equivalence of alternate modes of program delivery

TABLE 11.3 Possible Documentation Methods for the Library and Learning Resources Criteria

Review Focus	Examples of Documentation
Students' access to library resources	Hands-on training and continuing support provided to students; evaluation of training and support
Students' use of learning resources	Analysis of data regarding students' use of the appropriate learning resources
Laboratories, facilities, and equipment	Arrangements made to provide students with easy access to laboratories, facilities, and equipment; students' experience with these resources

TABLE 11.4 Possible Documentation Methods for the Student
Services Criteria

Review Focus	*Examples of Documentation*
Access to student services related to admissions, financial aid, academic advising, delivery of course materials, and placement and counseling	Policies and procedures related to each of the focus areas, how are they communicated, how are they implemented, and how the institution monitors their impact on program outcomes
Resolving student complaints	Records regarding the complaints received, what they dealt with, when and how they were addressed, and who was responsible for addressing them; what steps were taken to improve the services that received large numbers of complaints
Providing students with adequate and accurate information regarding the program, requirements, and available services	Explanation of strategies used to make essential information available to prospective learners, how these strategies are assessed, and how the assessment findings are used to make the needed modifications and adjustments; examples of publicity procedures and materials
Students have the knowledge and the equipment necessary to use the technology employed in the program and receive assistance if they experience difficulty in using it	Methods used to ensure that students possess the knowledge and equipment; self-instructional program designed to help students who are not familiar with the technology used to deliver the program

TABLE 11.5 Possible Documentation Methods for the Facilities and
Finances Criteria

Review Focus	Examples of Documentation
The institution possesses the equipment and technical expertise required for distance education	Description of the equipment available, the resources earmarked to upgrade the equipment on a regular basis, and technical expertise available to assist the faculty
Long-range planning, budgeting, and policy development processes reflect the resources essential to the viability and effectiveness of the program	Indication of how the distance program supports and extends institutional role and mission and how the needed policies and resources are integrated into institutional policies; documentation of the institution's financial and administrative commitment

References

American Association of University Professors. (2000). *Distance education and intellectual property issues* [Online]. Washington, DC: Author. Retrieved April 19, 2001, from the World Wide Web: www.aaup.org/DistncEd.htm

Council of Regional Accrediting Commissions. (2001). *Best practices for electronically offered degree and certificate programs* [Online]. Retrieved April 16, 2001, from the World Wide Web: www.ncahigherlearningcommission.org

Institute for Higher Education Policy. (2000). *Quality on the line.* Washington, DC: Author.

North Central Association of Colleges and Schools. (1997). *Handbook of accreditation* (2nd ed.). Chicago: Author.

Phipps, R. A., Wellman, J. V., & Merisotis, J. P. (1998). *Assuring quality in distance learning: A preliminary review.* Washington, DC: Council for Higher Education.

Sumler, D., & Zirkin, B. (1995, Spring). Interactive or non-interactive? That is the question: An annotated bibliography. *Journal of Distance Education, 10*(1), 95-112.

Conclusion

Distance education continues to grow at a dramatic pace. The expansion is driven by several factors, including

- The development of new computer and Internet technologies

- The increasing performance-to-price ratio of available computer technology

- The societal need for more educated and technically sophisticated employees

- The decreasing percentage of traditional-aged college students seeking higher education

- The emergence of for-profit educational enterprises

Some overly enthusiastic proponents of distance education have predicted the demise or withering of the traditional university or college. This will not come to pass. The cocurricular elements of a traditional on-campus undergraduate education (athletics, parties, dormitory life, and theater and musical performances, to name some) cannot be experienced any other way. But as we have seen, not all students seeking higher education desire, need, or can afford the cost of a traditional college experience. Hence, distance education makes it possible for institutions to fulfill their mission by serving an even wider population of learners. At the same time, the technology used in distance education is invigorating the on-campus experience as well. E-mail and Web-enhanced courses now afford instructors and students alike even more opportunities for interaction. Effective use of Web sites, chat rooms, and bulletin boards actually may *increase* the service that instructors can provide to students in large classes. Hence, we predict with some confidence that distance education will develop not as a competitor to traditional on-campus education but as another facet of it. At the same time, advances in distance education technology will enliven the on-campus classroom and provide instructors with even more tools for creative teaching.

Undoubtedly, new distance technologies will emerge and be combined with current ones. For example, as it becomes increasingly inexpensive to transfer large data files rapidly via the Internet (i.e., as the cost of increased bandwidth decreases), streaming video of high quality will come into wider use. It combines some of the advantages of video technology with Web-based technology and provides additional options for instruction.

The rapid rate at which delivery technology changes influenced the approach we took in writing this text. Our presentation has concentrated more on concepts, principles, and methodologies than on specific details about a given piece of equipment or instructional software. We believe that some of these principles will be more enduring than specific technologies. We hope that our exposition will help readers in designing, implementing, and assessing new ways of enhancing student learning. For us, learning includes engagement with peers and with the instructor—interaction that is fundamental to the educational process. Whether students are enrolled in an on-campus course or are taking the class at a distance, what matters is their engagement in reading, writing, discussing, and reflecting—the building blocks of active learning. It is less important what combination of technologies is used; what matters is the effectiveness of instructional strategies in fostering student learning. Although the quality assurance of distance learning programs tends to rely heavily on assessment of outcomes rather than on processes, outcomes depend on the processes. As we have emphasized throughout the text, the key ingredients in promoting student learning are the availability of the instructors and the intellectual engagement of the students. Thus, all accrediting agencies expect specific evidence not only regarding the learning outcomes but also regarding the interactions among the learners and between the learners and the instructors.

Distance education inevitably depends on technology for providing access to learning resources, for delivering instruction to learners, for promoting students' interaction with each other and with the instructor, and for facilitating communication between learners and support staff. Therefore, an institution starting a distance education program must allocate adequate resources for acquiring, maintaining, and upgrading the technology infrastructure. Also essential is an institutional commitment to providing the technical support that faculty and students need to make effective use of technology. Neither the technology nor user support is inexpensive, although both can be provided efficiently.

Higher education faculty differ widely in their knowledge of information technology and in their skill at putting it to work in the classroom. Indeed, a large fraction of today's college and university instructors received their graduate education when the current technology was not an integral part of their daily life. This is especially true for faculty members who earned their graduate degrees before the 1980s and the advent of personal computers. At the same time, the median age of students who enroll in distance programs is higher than for traditional on-campus programs: One recent report indicates that 25% of *all* undergraduate students are over age 30 and that 23% of *all* graduate students are over age 40 (National Center for Education Statistics, 1997, Table 175). In addition, many of the nontraditional students are place bound, do not have access to postsecondary education in their communities, have not had adequate exposure to technology in high school, and have limited resources to purchase and maintain a computer and the needed software.

In light of the above demographics, faculty members teaching a distance course for the first time need to be provided appropriate training related to both technical and curricular matters. If new technologies are added at a later date, further training will be required. Similarly, students must have the needed equipment and training required for a particular program and continuing access to technical support. Without such institutional commitment and support, it is simply not feasible for faculty to offer distance courses and for students to achieve the stipulated learning outcomes.

Distance learning places new demands on the faculty beyond the technological issues just described. The faculty role changes from being mainly a content expert to a combination of content expert, learning process design expert, and process implementation manager (Massy, 1997). The instructor also serves as a mentor, motivator, and interpreter. In addition, he or she also needs to be an "expert learner" who leads the learning process by personal example. What are the implications of this new set of expectations? We have already noted the need for providing continuing training and support related to technical and curricular matters. In addition, distance courses usually require instructors to spend substantial time preparing materials such as the syllabus, study guide, instructional units, reference lists, links to Web sites, assignments, and assessment procedures. Although this is not an exhaustive list of all the tasks instructors need to perform before they offer a distance course, it indicates the need to plan ahead and to budget adequate time in anticipation of making the course available to students at a distance. Recognizing that development of distance courses requires substantial time and effort, a number of private and federal agencies often make grant support available for innovative efforts. Because space constraints do not allow us to discuss grant-seeking strategies, we refer the interested reader to *The Distance Learning Funding Sourcebook* (Krebs, 1999), now in its fourth edition. Most agencies do not fund technology purchases; they fund content development, the curriculum.

The labor-intensive nature of teaching at a distance does not stop once the course has been designed. It continues once students start taking the course. Given the wide range of differences among learners, the individualized nature of their interactions with the faculty, and the need for personalized feedback on their assignments and exams, faculty must allocate adequate time to address student needs throughout the course. Because faculty members teaching distance courses are expected to maintain contact with all learners; provide students with detailed, personalized, and timely feedback; and offer individualized consultation and guidance, these activities create additional time demands. Administrators should take these increased expectations into consideration when determining class size and teaching load.

We have highlighted above some important challenges distance learning presents to an institution, its administrators, and its faculty. But why should academia make an effort to address these challenges? We believe that the underlying motivation is to serve students from different social, cultural, economic, and experiential backgrounds who for one reason or another have not been able to participate in postsecondary education. Although providing increased access to a full range of students is certainly a worthy goal, the question remains whether the higher education community has been successful in reaching those segments of the population that have been underrepresented in the past. To the best of our knowledge, the evidence in this regard is not conclusive. As we reported in Chapter 1 (Figure 1.2), in the United States only 6% of 2-year private colleges and 22% of 4-year private colleges offered distance learning courses in 1997-1998. Because many of these colleges serve a large number of minority populations (all the colleges located on the Indian Reservations are private 2-year colleges, and a large number of historically black colleges are private 4-year colleges), these statistics indicate that many members of minority communities may still have limited access to postsecondary education. A recent report from the College Board and the Institute for Higher Education Policy titled *The Virtual University and Educational Opportunity: Issues of Equity and Access for the Next Generation* (1999) also targets access as its theme. Focusing primarily on Internet-based distance learning courses, the report argues that information have-nots are at a distinct disadvantage when it comes to taking courses online. A major barrier for those who are underrepresented in higher education—African Americans, Hispanics, Native Americans—is the lack of computer or online services both in homes and in schools. The report recommends that government policymakers take steps to ensure equality in distance learning. Fortunately, a number of initiatives are currently under way to increase minority students' access to courses offered via distance learning.

One possible approach to promoting widespread access is the development of statewide or regional consortia of traditional institutions in which several colleges and universities jointly offer distance learning programs. Examples include the Education Network of Maine and the Southern Regional Electronic Campus. In addition to making education accessible to larger audiences from a wide geographical area, such arrangements have the potential to spread the initial development costs across many individual users. In other words, a collaborative arrangement may be an efficient approach for designing and offering distance programs because of the inherent economies of scale. At the time of this writing, such arrangements are still in their infancy, and hard data about their effectiveness and efficiency are not available. We do know, however, that a large number of other such arrangements and their variations are being developed to offer professional programs in fields such as engineering, business, nursing, and teacher education.

In addition to the consortia, community public libraries are beginning to play an important role in providing increased access to Web-based courses. Because many academic institutions are providing learners with access to scholarly journals, monographs, and other full-text resources in a networked environment, linking the public libraries with these institutions may make it convenient for place-bound learners to participate in distance programs. Furthermore, library reference and instructional services are becoming available electronically. In time, audio and video elements will enhance these services by bringing together the best aspects of face-to-face and electronic communications. Staff members at many libraries in the United States are exploring creative ways of providing learners with reference and research services electronically. Let us hope that as a result of these efforts, learners with limited resources will also be able to participate in distance programs of their choice.

Distance education has seen its greatest growth in wealthy, industrialized countries. The personal computer revolution and development of the World Wide Web have the potential to make distance learning truly international; unfortunately, the Third World is now finding itself on the other side of another wall, this time a digital one. Internationally, the United Nations Educational, Scientific, and Cultural Organization's (UNESCO) Division of Basic Education is supporting an initiative to bring together nine high-population countries to meet basic learning needs of those presently lacking access to educational services, to offer teacher training programs, and to reinforce the quality and capacity of formal education. In addition to UNESCO's work, a number of U.S. universities and colleges are making postsecondary education available through cooperative arrangements with institutions from other countries. The development of high-quality wireless communication networks offers even remote areas a chance to access the Internet, but substantial capital investment will be required to make computers and cell phone technology available to the poorer countries. For us, distance education will have fulfilled its potential when people all over the world can access the tools for learning. We trust that that day does not lie in the distant future.

References

College Board and Institute for Higher Education Policy. (1999). *The virtual university and educational opportunity: Issues of equity and access for the next generation* [Online]. Retrieved April 19, 2001, from the World Wide Web: www.collegeboard.org/policy/html/virtual.html

Krebs, A. (1999). *The distance learning funding sourcebook*. Dubuque, IA: Kendall/ Hunt.

Massy, W. F. (1997). Life on the wired campus: How information technology will shape institutional futures. In D. G. Oblinger & S. C. Rush (Eds.), *The learning revolution: The challenge of information technology in the academy*. Bolton, NY: Anker.

National Center for Education Statistics. (1997). *Integrated postsecondary education enrollment, 1995 survey* [Online]. Washington, DC: U.S. Department of Education. Retrieved April 19, 2001, from the World Wide Web: www.nces.ed.gov/pubs/digest97/d97t175.html

Author Index

Subject Index

About the Authors

Chandra Mohan Mehrotra is Professor of Psychology and Dean for Special Projects at The College of St. Scholastica. He is a Fellow of the American Psychological Association and is the recipient of several awards for teaching and service. He is a Consulting Editor for *Teaching of Psychology* and serves on the editorial board of *Educational Gerontology*. He has published numerous articles, edited *Teaching and Aging* (1984), coauthored *Aging and Diversity* (1998), and served as guest editor for a special issue of *Educational Gerontology* (1996). He has designed distance learning courses in introductory statistics, research methods, program evaluation, and aging and diversity and provided leadership in the development of a master of education program that is offered via distance learning. He has presented papers and symposia on distance learning at annual meetings of the American Psychological Association, the North Central Association of Colleges and Schools, and the Gerontological Society of America. His activities related to teaching improvement, faculty development, and program evaluation have been supported by major grants from the National Science Foundation,

241

the Bush Foundation, the Blandin Foundation, and the Kellogg Foundation. He is currently directing a research training program for psychology faculty, with support from the National Institute on Aging in the National Institutes of Health.

C. David Hollister is Professor in the School of Social Work at the University of Minnesota. Since 1993, he has been actively involved in the development and accreditation of the school's master of social work distance education program, and he teaches distance courses on community practice methods and on substance abuse. He has published a number of articles evaluating distance education and has presented papers on distance education at meetings of the Council on Social Work Education, at the annual University of South Carolina Conference on Educational Technology in Social Work, and at international conferences. He is Associate Secretary General for the Inter-University Consortium for International Social Development and is a member of the editorial board of *Social Development Issues*. In addition to distance education, his research interests include the evaluation of welfare reform, the evaluation of substance abuse treatment, and the use of geographic information systems in neighborhood revitalization. His research and teaching activities have been supported by the Blandin Foundation, the Joyce Foundation, the Bush Foundation, and the National Institute on Alcohol Addiction and Abuse.

Lawrence McGahey is Associate Professor, Chair of the Chemistry Department, and Chair of the Natural Sciences Division at The College of St. Scholastica. He has been involved in the development of St. Scholastica's distance education program as a member of the Graduate Council and Graduate Curriculum Committee. In addition, he has experience in developing and incorporating Web-based instructional materials into science courses. His research and teaching efforts have been supported by the National Science Foundation, the Research Corporation, and the U.S. Department of Education. He is also a manuscript reviewer and annotator for the *Journal of Chemical Education*.